The Outside Story

The Outside Story

local writers explore the **nature**
of Vermont and New Hampshire

edited by Chuck Wooster
Northern Woodlands magazine

WITH ILLUSTRATIONS BY ADELAIDE TYROL

Northern Woodlands
PO Box 471
Corinth, Vermont 05039
802.439.6292

For bulk sales or ordering information, call 1-800-290-5232 or visit www.northernwoodlands.org.

Printed in the United States of America by Thomson-Shore, Inc., a member of the Green Press Initiative, on paper with 30% post-consumer recycled content and vegetable-based inks.

Designed and composed by Jenna Dixon, Bookbuilder
Copyedited by Sue Kashanski
Proofread by Marian Cawley
Index by Jan Williams

ISBN 0-9786599-0-2

First printing, 2006

1   2   3   4   5   06   07   08   09   10

This collection of essays is dedicated to Marguerite Wellborn, writer, naturalist, and philanthropist, whose extraordinary generosity has touched the lives of thousands of people across New Hampshire and Vermont.

Marguerite Wellborn spent most of her childhood on a hill farm in the Mohawk River watershed of New York state, an environment short on playmates but rich in natural woodlands and wild and domestic animals. Here she first experienced, and began to respect and cherish, the ecology of our planet. All her life, she loved merely to witness, and to feel connected with, the web of life that she once described as "beautifully simple and awesomely complex."

Her personal bent was scholarly, so she not only spent time observing the daily activities of many species but also memorized taxonomies, studied what other scholars had discovered, and sent out this news via her succinct and elegant prose.

Her assumption that education can illuminate human decisions, and her fear that human ignorance of biological systems will inevitably destroy them, motivated her to establish the Wellborn Ecology Fund. At an advanced age, when her personal energy was failing but her financial resources had greatly increased, she offered this gift to the residents of Vermont and New Hampshire with the hope that it would diminish ignorance and increase a sense of responsibility for the web of life.

She would have been delighted by the essays that fill this inspiring book.

Sally Wellborn
JULY 25, 2006

Contents

A Natural Legacy for New Hampshire and Vermont

◌

Steve Taylor

Early in 2000, staff members at the Upper Valley Region of the New Hampshire Charitable Foundation (then known as Upper Valley Community Foundation) received a call from a local law firm. Marguerite Wellborn, a resident of the Kendal retirement community in Hanover, New Hampshire, and a client of the law firm, had recently passed away. Her will named the Foundation as a beneficiary:

> I give, devise and bequeath the remainder of my estate to be called the Wellborn Ecology Fund to be used for public awareness of environmental and ecological issues in the Upper Valley [of New Hampshire and Vermont] primarily through educational facilities such as, but not limited to, the Montshire Museum and public or private schools, and also to encourage independent study and action by individuals in the form of grants.

With these few lines, Marguerite Wellborn made a remarkable and lasting gift to the Connecticut Valley region of New Hampshire and Vermont. She endowed the people of this region with resources to promote the study of nature and the interaction between humans and the natural world around them. Her legacy—the Wellborn Ecology Fund—was created within the Foundation to promote environmental and ecological education and knowledge.

In 2001, the Foundation established a grant-making program for the Wellborn Ecology Fund to support ecology—education programs that focus on the 61 communities in the Connecticut River valley of west-central New Hampshire and east-central Vermont. These programs provide Upper Valley residents with the knowledge, experience, skills, and understanding to make informed decisions and take useful actions aimed at protecting and sustaining the natural systems of the region. The goals of the Wellborn Ecology Fund are to build on a strong local and regional sense of place, turn people on to nature, increase ecological understanding, strengthen the regional environmental network, and improve regional environmental education.

We are pleased to report that, between 2001 and 2006, more than $2 million in grants and contracts have been awarded by the Wellborn Ecology Fund to organizations in New Hampshire and Vermont for their work in the Upper Valley. Marguerite Wellborn placed her trust in the Foundation, and we have worked ever since to turn her vision of ecological literacy into reality for the people of this region.

Mrs. Wellborn was herself an avid naturalist with an enduring passion for studying and protecting the natural world. She believed that teaching people to appreciate our natural systems and to understand their scientific underpinnings were crucial first steps toward developing the attitudes and skills necessary to protect and conserve those systems.

In addition to being a naturalist, Mrs. Wellborn was also a nature writer. In her hometown of Schenectady, New York, she penned a regular ecology column. That tradition continued when she retired, with her stories and essays on bugs, birds, and other topics published in the *Kendal Times*.

To honor her nature-writing tradition, the Wellborn Ecology Fund commissioned the staff of *Northern Woodlands* in Corinth, Vermont, to develop a weekly series of articles on nature topics for publication in local newspapers. The articles, written by a variety of local authors and accompanied by black and white line drawings, follow the seasons' ebb and flow across the region. In addition to exploring natural history, the goal of these articles is to examine the linkages and interactions between the human species and the rest of the natural world. The articles are intended to inform, educate, and inspire, telling the "why" as well as the "what" and "how" of the world around us.

Since 2002, these articles have appeared in daily and weekly newspapers across the twin states. We have collected our favorites here for your reading pleasure, and we hope you enjoy them. We are fortunate to live in an area of such natural beauty and fortunate to have people like Marguerite Wellborn remind us of how extraordinary our corner of the world is. ∽

STEVE TAYLOR is the commissioner of the New Hampshire Department of Agriculture, Markets & Food and the advisory board chair of the Upper Valley region of the New Hampshire Charitable Foundation.

Preface

❦

Chuck Wooster

As I recollect, I was standing in the pouring rain watching some college students compete in a wood-chopping competition when Kevin Peterson of the New Hampshire Charitable Foundation came up to me, pulled the raincoat back from my ear, and said, "Hey—I have an idea. Let's put together an ecology article series for the newspapers."

"Great!" I said, brimming with the confidence and enthusiasm that can only come from never having done something before. And of the chance to step inside out of the rain.

That day was more than five years ago. Since then, the collaboration between Kevin's employer, the New Hampshire Charitable Foundation, and mine, Northern Woodlands, has produced an ongoing series of ecology articles that appear each week in newspapers across New Hampshire and Vermont. The book that you are holding in your hand is a collection of our favorite articles from the first four years.

What we're offering you with these essays is this: the inside scoop on the outside story. Local writers examining local subjects. Collectively, these essays provide a broad look at the ecology of Vermont and New Hampshire today. We hope that readers in adjacent states and provinces will also find ideas of interest in this book, but our overall goal is to present a series of essays, grouped by month, that discuss ecological happenings in this one particular corner of the globe.

Are you sitting in front of the woodstove right now, wondering how those poor critters outside manage to stay warm? There's an article for you on animal fur in January. Is it spring, and a danged woodpecker keeps rapping on your stovepipe at 6 in the morning? There's an article about that in May. Are you wondering if acid rain is still a problem here in New Hampshire and Vermont? Several authors offer perspectives on the topic.

We're not intending for this book to be the last word or the exhaustive text. But we do promise that it will be a lively read and that you'll remember something when you're done. So whatever the season, we invite you to kick back, open the book, thumb through it, and enjoy an essay or two. ❧

Acknowledgments

❧

Every book requires a bunch of capable hands to transform a rough idea into bound pages. Here are a few of the hands behind this book.

Marguerite Wellborn, whose generosity has made the Wellborn Ecology Series, and this book, possible.

Kevin Peterson of the New Hampshire Charitable Foundation, who had the original idea for both the article series and this book and who has championed both since day one.

Julia Olivares, communications and marketing director for the Foundation, who asked helpful questions about the book's purpose, audience, and design.

The Wellborn Ecology Fund Advisory Committee—Megan Camp, Lisa Cashdan, Karen Harris, John Hawkins, Thelma Hewitt, Mike McGean, Nory Parr, Bruce Schwaegler, Sylvia Sivret, and Fred Thomas—who supported the article series and whose thoughtful analysis strengthened the final product.

The editorial staff at Northern Woodlands—Anne Margolis, Virginia Barlow, and Stephen Long—who grappled with every article and made each of them better.

Virginia Barlow, in particular, whose collection of calendar entries opens each chapter.

Adelaide Tyrol, illustrator extraordinaire, whose work brings the articles to life and gives the book a visual consistency.

The two dozen authors whose work appears in this book and who, without exception, made the deadlines on time.

Sue Kashanski, copy editor and provider of perspective, who waded through more than 200 articles to create the coherent collection that appears in these pages.

Finally, Jenna Dixon, book designer and production manager, who transformed the electronic words into bound pages, and did so with infectious flair and creativity. ❧

The Outside Story

Introduction

❧

Willem Lange

Many years ago, Robert Frost wrote, in "Birches": "Earth's the right place for love: I don't know where it's likely to go better." Ever since I first read that, I've used the second half of the line to refer to this beautiful part of the world—Vermont, New Hampshire, and the adjacent corners of the North Woods. It's especially helpful in March, when the sun brightens, the ice remains hard as steel in our dooryard, and my wife and I dream of southern climates. It's then I resort to that refrain.

I don't know where it's likely to go better.

Last Sunday morning broke cool, gray, and raining. But there was a stir in the air, suggesting an imminent change in the weather; all through church, I kept checking the stained glass window on the east wall above the altar, expecting that any minute it would blaze into life. No soap. Twelve o'clock came and went, and so did we, driving home on wet roads through wet, brown, bare woods.

The change, a mild cold front, came at midafternoon, the warm sun breaking through torn clouds to draw the rain back up and set a partridge booming in the swamp. I took a look at the pile of work on my desk, dredged up a quotation to justify what I was about to do ("The Sabbath was made for Man, not Man for the Sabbath."), and dug my favorite fishing rod out of the closet.

The pond, when I got there, was glassy as glycerin, and cold, just getting used to being liquid again. Last year's grass lay brown and flat around the muddy verge. The songs of red-winged blackbirds chirred and burbled in the cattails, and the bleating of spring lambs floated down from the pasture above. The sun hung a little above a spruce plantation to the west, just beginning to cast pointed shadows across the water. As I set my little canoe down at the edge, a large trout slurped at the surface about one hundred feet out. The ring of ripples spread slowly and died away.

Fifty years earlier, that would have had me out on the pond like a shot. This idyll would not have been complete till I had caught and killed at least one fish, for I considered it a failure to "get skunked." Not any more. There was absolutely no rush. This was perfect just the way it was, and the failure of anything more to happen would not diminish that a bit.

I'd brought a Snickers bar with me, an indulgence permitted by my missing supper. As I unwrapped it, a flash of color and a slight movement in the alders to my right caught my eye. I turned toward it. A gorbie!—or whiskey jack, or camp robber, or moose bird, or Canada jay, or gray jay, or *Geai gris. Perisoreus canadensis*, if you like. The name doesn't matter. They're favorites of mine, and I love to see them around. Symbols of the deep woods, and reputed by the old-timers to be the spirits of dead loggers, they'll pick up anything edible that isn't nailed down and come right to your hand—or even the top of your head—for a treat. Men in the logging camps sometimes fed them bits of bread soaked in whiskey to watch them get tipsy; but to injure one was sure to evoke a curse. I'd thought they'd all disappeared from this neck of the woods, but here was one, and he must have had his eye on me, to be on the spot as soon as I stopped. As I watched, his mate settled silently on a branch near him.

I broke off a chunk of the bar, ate most of it, and spread out my left hand with a small piece on the palm. He came down first—dry little claws gripping my fingers—picked up the offering, and flew back into the trees to eat it. Then it was a piece for the lady, and as soon as she was gone, he was back, watching expectantly. I repeated the routine; but this time he made a pass at the main bar, wrapper and all, in my other hand. So I stuck it into my pocket, rationed it out, and we dined there, daintily, the three of us, till the Snickers was gone. Then I turned back to the canoe.

A very small thing—much like the snow shaken down upon Robert Frost once by a crow in a hemlock tree—but so much a part of these North Woods: a silent conversation between two species at home in the forest. I stepped into the canoe. The conversation was over, and each of us turned to his evening affairs.

In these days of increased environmental consciousness, I am more than ever aware how few—and ever fewer—are the places like this. Looking about me in every direction, I could see literally nothing that still existed in its natural, created state, except the shape of the glacier-sculpted mountains across the valley. Yet I was surrounded by the results of good stewardship—hayfields, pastures, timberland, the pond, scattered houses and barns—land that sustains and refreshes because it in its turn has not been misused and exhausted. In the next couple of weeks, pairs of ducks will begin dropping by for the night on their way north. Up on the hill, there are bluebird houses tacked to fence posts around the pasture; in the mud beside my own big tracks are the prints of deer stooping to drink and raccoons hunting crayfish in the shallows.

I paddled out onto the pond. I've always considered the first cast of each fishing season to be portentous and so take care in its location and preparation. This time I used a glistening black fly named a Crystal Bugger. Not far from where I'd seen the rise a few minutes before, I laid it out into the middle of a shadowed lobe of the pond, let it sink, and gave it a twitch.

It would be easy, here at the lovely heart of one of the loveliest parts of the Northeast, to forget the distress of much of the rest of the earth—to suppose that one, looking from space, would see millions of elderly men fishing quietly in still ponds on a Sunday evening. But I've too often seen the incredible human arrogance and devastation of Hydro-Quebec; the miles of blasted, poisoned, orphaned earth in north Jersey and eastern Kentucky; the once-lovely Androscoggin staining the Gulf of Maine; the oceanside clear-cuts of the Pacific Northwest; and the haze of industrial pollution over the Arctic Ocean.

The collection of essays in your hands is a pretty good summary of the state of affairs hereabouts. Some of them will help you forget—essays that glimpse the rare beauty of the place and examine the plants and animals

4

that share our neighborhood. And there are articles that will certainly help you remember. Despite the marvels of our place and time, acid rain, mercury poisoning, and a warming climate are still very much with us—not just in the wider world, but right here on our own patch of ground. Taken together, these essays are a celebration of people and nature together; not as together, perhaps, as in the days of hardscrabble farms and logging camps and travel on horseback, but more together, in all likelihood, than will be the case when our children and their children happen across these words.

Back at the pond, my ceremonial first cast did not elicit a strike. No matter. A few more casts, a rise here and there, the faint mist from an evening cold front. We brooded awhile together, the water and I. The canoe drifted across the surface in the light air with its graying fisherman, at large in a local wilderness. The wilderness in turn no more than a basin of water tucked between pastures and woodlots.

I don't know where it's likely to go better. ∾

January

❧

FIRST WEEK

Shaking the tall, straight stalks of mullein will release
a shower of tiny, black seeds on the snow.

Beneath the ice, some aquatic plants are
photosynthesizing, even at low temperatures
and light levels. This produces much-needed
oxygen for fish and other organisms.

Little piles of seeds in the woodpile or in the
toes of shoes may be the work of deer mice.

Retired Christmas trees propped up
near the birdfeeder will provide birds with
shelter and some protection from the wind.

SECOND WEEK

January 10, 1998: "The Great Ice Storm."

Bad weather will send American tree sparrows
to birdfeeders. In normal times, they prefer
self-reliance and feed on weed seeds.

A pile of ruffed grouse feathers on the
snow may be the work of a goshawk.

Look for common mergansers
and common goldeneye ducks on
ice-free sections of large rivers.

Meadow voles breed almost all year round.
Fortunately, they are eaten year-round, too, and
are the major food now of hawks and owls.

THIRD WEEK

January 20: St. Agnes Eve, when, according to tradition, winter's bitter cold gives way to warmer weather.

Ivory-colored poison ivy seeds are still on the vine—nutritious food for many birds.

Woodland jumping mice and meadow jumping mice hibernate below the frost line, curled in tight balls.

Coyotes form pair bonds in winter, and they may be pretty vocal about it.

Chickadees in the cattails are likely to be feeding on cattail moth larvae, not the infinitesimally small cattail seeds.

FOURTH WEEK

The temperature of hibernating woodchucks is now about 40° Fahrenheit. Their hearts are beating just 3 to 10 times a minute.

Cedar swamps provide cover and a favorite food source for deer. Moose don't like cedar; for them, it's starvation food.

If mice find their way into your house, weasels may come looking for them.

Evening grosbeaks may be feeding in boxelders, the only maple to hold its seeds through winter.

Bear cubs are born. Each of the two or three babies weighs 0.4 to 0.7 pounds.

Winter Woods are Not So Empty

Stephen Long

As you stand poised at the edge of the winter woods, it may be hard to imagine that within that stark, white, silent landscape, the resident animals are going about their routine of finding food and shelter. While the woods may seem to be asleep, a walk through them will show many signs of life.

Snow dampens any sounds you make walking, so you have a great opportunity to see wildlife, especially if you follow the lead of deer hunters: walk a few steps, and then stop and look in all directions, even back toward where you've been.

One of the tricks is to use your eyes not as a telephoto lens, but as a wide angle. Don't peer, just keep your eyes awake and alert for movement—much of what you see will first be noticed out of the corner of your eye.

More than likely, your first glimpse will be of a step or the movement of a tail or an ear—you probably won't see an entire profile of a deer or a fox. If you see the animal before it sees you, freeze in position and you might get to watch for a good long time. Many mammals rely more heavily on their sense of smell than on their vision, and if your scent doesn't reach them, they won't spook. Deer, for instance, can stare in your direction from as close as 30

yards, but if your scent doesn't give you away, they won't detect you unless you move. On the other hand, turkeys have extraordinarily keen vision and can detect the slightest movement, even a blink of an eye.

What species might you see? It's easier to start with those you won't see: the migrators, such as waterfowl, many of the raptors, and most of the songbirds will be gone; and the mammals that den up for the winter—beaver, bear, woodchuck, skunk, raccoon, and chipmunk—will be invisible.

But that leaves all sorts of other birds and mammals. You just need to know where to look because the likelihood of seeing a particular species varies with the terrain and the vegetation. Winter is a great time to venture out into swampy areas that are inaccessible when the ground isn't frozen. You'll likely see the work of beavers and their dome-shaped lodge, within which as many as a dozen beavers will be denned up for the winter with a cache of branches.

Otters stay active all winter, and you may see one galumphing along a river bank or swimming in open water. In the bottomlands, you might also come across the mink, who is never far from water. Its smaller cousin, the weasel, will be harder to see because it molts to a white coat in winter. If the area is brushy enough, you could see a red fox or coyote padding quietly in pursuit of dinner.

If the woods are thick with young softwoods about the size of Christmas trees, the dinner the fox or coyote is after could be the snowshoe hare, which will also be sporting its white winter coat. And if there is some agricultural land nearby, you have a good chance of seeing a flock of wild turkeys. They will be down from the ridges, scratching for seeds, hibernating insects, and undigested corn kernels from manure piles.

On the forested slopes, the softwoods provide a safe haven for many species. A thick stand of evergreens creates its own microclimate with less snow depth, diminished winds, and slightly warmer temperatures. If deer are about, their trails may be so worn that they look as if a dairy herd uses them. Even though you may not see the deer, they are in there. Don't push them, because you'll make them waste much-needed energy in running from you.

From the safe heights of the softwood trees, red squirrels may squawk at you. If there are hemlock branches littered on the ground, look up and you might see a porcupine. Its nemesis, the fisher, could be traveling on the ground or climbing trees.

Many animals prefer the transition zone between softwoods and hardwoods. Here, you are likely to find gray squirrels and winter birds like woodpeckers, chickadees, blue jays, and evening grosbeaks. You could see an owl take off from its perch high in a pine and fly silently through the upper story.

In the hardwood stands, it's easier to see and to travel, and for that reason, prey animals are less likely to be showing themselves. One that might surprise you—literally—is the ruffed grouse, particularly in the vicinity of its favorite food source, the aspen. You'll know it's a grouse when it bursts out of the snow in a wild beating of wings that leaves your heart pounding.

And here you thought the winter woods were silent and empty! ∽

Watch It—Hot Rocks

Chuck Wooster

It's an odorless, colorless gas; you can't see it, smell it, or taste it. As one wag once put it, it's just the thing to require a bunch of government regulation.

But it's also the number one cause of lung cancer for nonsmokers. The villain in question is radon, a radioactive gas released by uranium in our rocks and soils that finds its way into our basements, wells, and houses. If you breathe in enough of it over time, chances are it'll do you no good.

Wait a minute, uranium? In New Hampshire and Vermont? Yep. Uranium isn't locally abundant only in Seabrook and Vernon. Uranium is, in fact, quite common in the ground beneath our feet—not in the concentrations required to make a bomb or power a reactor, but more than enough to make its presence known.

Uranium is a large element, much larger than the common elements in the majority of our rocks, such as silicon, calcium, oxygen, and even iron. It's too big to fit into the crystals that hold these other elements, and so it tends to be left until the last minute when crystals are forming in molten rock. At that point, the other crystals just sort of brick around the uranium to hold it in place.

If uranium is one of the last kids picked for the mineral team, then granite is one of the last kids picked for the rock team—it tends to be formed by the dregs of molten rock.

Perhaps you can see where this is leading: uranium is left to the end when minerals are forming, granite is left to the end when rocks are forming out of minerals, and hence uranium and granite often go together. We have a lot of granite in New Hampshire and Vermont, and now you get the picture.

At the dawn of the nuclear age, there was talk of mining uranium from the famous pink Conway granite of the White Mountains. But like gold, another large element that doesn't easily fit in with our common elements, uranium is rarely mined straight out of igneous rock. Instead, geologists look for places where erosion, hydrothermal activity, or other natural processes have concentrated uranium into enriched deposits. States in the American West like Wyoming are famous for these areas; states in New England are not.

But if uranium has been under our feet for millions of years around here, how come radon has only recently been added to the lineup of villains? The answer, in part, is apparent to anyone who has ever lived in an old house—ventilation. Only a generation or two ago, most of us worked outside much of the time, lived in drafty houses, and drank water from shallow, dug wells. These days, most of us work inside, insulate our houses as best we can, and, if we need well water, we drill wells hundreds of feet deep into the bedrock to get it. Radon gas seeps in through our foundations or hitches a ride in with the well water, and the result is that radon can be trapped and concentrated in our houses and businesses.

It is common (though not legally required) these days for buildings to be tested for radon whenever they change hands. If your house hasn't ever been tested, you might want to look into it. The radon hot spot in Vermont is the southern Green Mountains, where the granitic roots of the mountain range are exposed. In New Hampshire it's the White Mountain area, with its multi-aged, granite-family bedrock. But your results may vary; not all granite emits radon, and not all radon comes from granite.

Back to the Conway granite for a moment. Although radon may be undetectable to the human eyes and nose, uranium can be indirectly observed throughout the White Mountains, especially in the east. Hold a fresh chunk of this pinkish rock up to your eye for a moment—don't worry, there isn't *that* much uranium in it—and you'll see three distinct minerals: a pink one (feldspar), a black one (mica), and a gray one (quartz).

Quartz crystals are usually clear like glass, not gray. There is enough uranium in Conway granite—in this case, bricked in with the black mica crystals—that tens of millions of years of radiation have distorted the quartz crystals so much that they no longer transmit light very well. The result is called "smoky quartz" and is clear proof that there is uranium in the rock. And also proof that this whole radon business isn't a government conspiracy. ∿

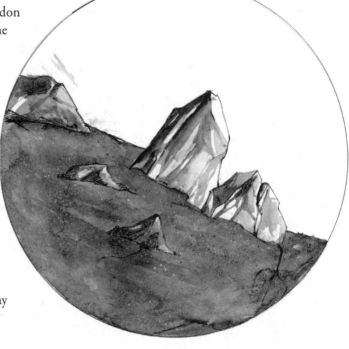

Tiny Warrior

Ted Levin

Istood still as the weasel rippled, white and lustrous, through the stone wall. Six feet away, a deer mouse—whose footfalls must have aroused the weasel—cowered against a tussock of grass. Suddenly, the mouse burst to the right, then froze. Stung by the sound, the weasel hit the ground in a dead run. She held the mouse's convoluted trail with her nose to the earth like a bloodhound, twice passing within inches of the mouse itself. But the mouse never flinched, and the weasel pressed on.

As the weasel finally closed in, the mouse bolted. Simultaneously, the weasel screeched and continued the pursuit, a tiny warrior with inexhaustible concentration. They darted across a mat of leaves, across a shag of fern, along a length of fallen elm limb. Both animals merged in a blur, the weasel furiously kicking and scratching and wrapping snake-like around the helpless mouse. When teeth met skull, all struggling ceased, and the weasel, with prey in mouth, disappeared back into the stone wall.

There are three weasel species in North America, two of which live hereabouts: the long-tailed, and the smaller short-tailed, or ermine. Collectively, they are quintessential mouse predators, sometimes following their prey into rural homes. I have live-trapped weasels behind a refrigerator in Norwich, Vermont, a stove in West Hartford, Vermont, and a furnace in Enfield, New Hampshire. In St. Johnsbury, Vermont, during the winter of 1987, several residents reported ermines in their homes. The fall of 1985 had produced a bumper crop of acorns and beechnuts and seeds. And after the high production of nutritious food, there followed a high production of nutritious mice. When the mouse population is up, more weasels survive the winter. Since a weasel can go anywhere a mouse can go, if snow forces mice inside, hungry weasels will follow.

One St. Johnsbury man caught an ermine in his living room and released it on the hill behind his house. The next night it was back. He reset the trap, and re-caught the weasel. This happened again and again. Eventually, he drove the weasel six miles away and released it. That night, the man again caught a weasel. He was sure it was the same one he had released. Of course, no one else believed him; a small mammal only twelve inches long surely cannot cover six miles in a single night, past a corner of St. Johnsbury, past owls and cats and fishers (which eat weasels), and past cars (which flatten them). The man needed proof, so the next night he caught the weasel and marked it with a spot of green nail polish and again released it six miles from home. In the morning, he checked his trap and found a weasel—ermine white with a black-tipped tail and a green spot on its rump. Finally, he drove the weasel twelve miles away and set it free. Although the record for the longest distance traveled by a short-tailed weasel is 21.6 miles, that record trip required seven months. The St. Johnsbury weasel did not return.

Of the three species of North American weasels, the long-tailed is the largest. Males are 18 inches long, including a six-and-a-half-inch tail, and weigh about eight ounces. Females are four inches shorter and less than half the weight. Besides leopards in the Old World, mountain lions in the New World, and man in both worlds, long-tailed weasels have the most extensive north-south distribution of any wild mammal. From southern Canada to Peru, they pursue rats, mice, squirrels, gophers, rabbits, and sometimes day-old piglets.

Short-tailed weasels, which are much more common in our area, are circumpolar, ranging throughout northern Eurasia, where they're called stoats, and Canada, south into the northern-tier states, and west into the mountains. In both species of weasel, decreasing daylight triggers the autumn molt. The timing, however, is seldom precise and varies between species, within species, and even from year to year for the same individual. As nights grow longer, days shorter, and the maples begin to blush, the diminished light falling on a weasel's eyes causes the pituitary gland—the body's master

chemist—to signal the pineal gland. In most northern weasels, the pineal gland secretes *melatonin*, which alerts the central nervous system to stop the production of *melanin*, a dark pigment found in hair follicles. Thus, new hairs turn white.

I stood by the stone wall in the moonlight and squeaked for the weasel, hoping it would put the mouse aside and investigate the new sound, for weasels are intensely curious. This weasel never fell for my ruse—it had already left the area. A neat set of paired footprints showed that it had bounded away, the mouse in its mouth scraping the snow on either side of the weasel's head. ∿

Winter Fur

Anne Margolis

We humans are pretty lucky when it comes to winter. When the temperature plunges to 20 below, we can venture bravely forth clad in our stylish new slim-puffy jackets and Ugg boots. But what about all the other critters out there? The ones whose only protection from the meat locker of winter northern woods is the hair on their hides? Well, they have . . . the hair on their hides. But that hair has evolved some neat adaptations to fend off frigid temperatures.

Most of the animals that haven't flown south or holed up in a cozy den are endowed with fat, feathers, and fur that bulk up as winter approaches. Fat both insulates and serves as a food reserve when foraging is lean. By remaining extremely inactive, some animals, like raccoons, maintain such slow metabolisms that they can live exclusively off stored fat all winter. Feathers and fur, though, are an animal's first line of defense.

Birds that stick around New Hampshire and Vermont, like blue jays, chickadees, and goldfinches, set about growing more insulating down feathers as winter approaches. Chickadees will grow a coat that's 25 percent thicker than their summer wear. On cold days, birds fluff up these feathers to trap body heat. They look about as bulky as we do with five layers on, though cuter.

Most mammals sport a soft undercoat as well as a thicker, coarser overcoat. The undercoat serves to insulate, and it grows thicker in winter. This process is triggered by shortening days rather than dropping temperatures. Growth of the winter coat is preceded by shedding of the summer coat, a process that works in reverse in spring. (Humans shed seasonally too—one more reason to launder those sheets at least twice a year.) The overcoat is made up of guard hairs, which repel snow, absorb heat from the sun, and trap heat that escapes through the undercoat.

Deer and moose have especially effective overcoats; they are the only mammals with *hollow* guard hairs, which have exceptional insulating qualities. According to tracker Susan Morse, it is not uncommon to come across a deer with a dusting of snow on its back that is not melted by the body's warmth. The synergy between the deer's undercoat (completely shed in the spring) and the guard hairs creates such effective insulation that the snow on its back stays frozen.

Moose guard hairs, says Morse, collect and transmit the sun's energy into the dense undercoat, where the dark-colored skin further absorbs the warmth, resulting in an elevation of skin surface temperature. "This layer of warmth," she says, "is then retained by the woolly undercoat, which in effect creates a warm-air insulating layer that minimizes loss of heat from the body core." She adds that biologists have observed captive moose in Alaska that don't shiver even as temperatures reach 50° below zero!

Otters, while lacking hollow guard hairs, have a coat that seems tailor-made for their semi-aquatic lifestyle, even in winter. Biologists have calculated that in just one square inch of otter coat, there are around 400,000 hairs. What makes this thick coat so special, says Morse, is the impenetrability of the otter's woolly undercoat in tandem with its waterproof outer coat. The guard hairs of the outer coat are not only linked to each other via interlocking scales but also crimped in order to retain more warm air. As otters dive into the water, all this warm air is squeezed out of the coat, which Morse says is easily observed in the mass of air bubbles radiating from the swimming animal.

In order to reloft their coats, otters must constantly groom and dry themselves. This maintenance takes place at haul-outs—packed areas of snow on the shores of ponds where otters dwell. According to Morse, these areas are almost always south- or southwest-facing protected spots that provide optimal conditions for otters to absorb and retain the sun's warmth in preparation for the next dive.

Braving frigid air and water, otters just might be at the opposite end of the cold-tolerance scale from people. Having long ago lost our thick coats of winter fur (though not, perhaps, winter fat), we're fortunate to be able to compensate with artificial undercoats and overcoats—longjohns and parkas—of synthetic materials and also the tried-and-true coats of our wild cousins, the down and wool and even fur that keeps us toasty warm through the cold days and long nights of a northern winter. ⌒

Seeing Green in Winter

Carrie Chandler

Have you ever been walking through the woods on a snowy afternoon and seen a bit of green poking up through the snow? Seeing the green fronds of a fern at this time of year may seem like an uncommon occurrence, but there are actually three common evergreen ferns that survive in the harsh cold of a northern New England winter. Seeing one brings to mind the question: why do some ferns choose to stay green while most others have shed their leaves for the winter?

The simple answer to this question is that evergreen ferns want to get a jump-start on photosynthesis. Staying green throughout the winter gives them a few more weeks of photosynthesis in the early spring before other plants leaf out. They are also able to conduct photosynthesis longer in the fall, after the leaves on other plants have fallen to the ground.

Despite the advantage of a longer growing season, most of our local fern species are deciduous and lose their leaves in the fall. That's because the benefits of a longer period of photosynthesis bring with them some costs. Because evergreen fern fronds stay green throughout the winter, they must be able to withstand harsh temperatures and the increased likelihood of predation by winter-starved animals. Fern fronds in winter are relatively tough and have less nutritional value than in the summer, so the cost to an animal of digesting an evergreen leaf usually outweighs the nutritional benefit. But this may not stop a starving animal from tasting the fare. Some evergreen ferns go so far as to give off noxious fumes to deter predators from sampling their leaves.

Unappetizing leaves are not the only defense that evergreen ferns need to survive the winter. Unlike deciduous plants, evergreens must have leaves that are able to tolerate temperatures well below freezing, especially during those first few harsh days of winter before they are buried under the snow. Once there is a thick covering of snow on the ground, the leaves are protected in a comfortable, 32°F blanket.

Deciduous plants, faced with impending winter, pull as much sugar in from their leaves as possible before abandoning them to wither and fall off. Evergreen plants do just the opposite. As the days shorten, evergreens begin to store ever more sugar in their leaves. The sugar serves as antifreeze, protecting the leaves as temperatures fall 5° to 10° below freezing. When the temperature drops still further, the plants resort to the same method used by insects that survive in deep cold: stopping the formation of ice crystals in their tracks.

Ice begins with a single frozen crystal and then grows as other ice crystals bond with the first. Evergreens stop this growth by synthesizing antifreeze proteins that bind with the initial ice crystal and block the bonding of other crystals. In our part of New England, this mechanism will protect a plant down to around −20° Fahrenheit. In other regions, where the temperature can stay below −20° Fahrenheit for many weeks, even evergreens will freeze solid. They withstand this temperature extreme by evacuating all the water from their cells, insuring that, when ice crystals do form, they end up outside the cell walls, preventing the cells from rupturing.

In deep winter, when evergreens are using these mechanisms to prevent freezing, photosynthesis halts. If it didn't, the process would create free radicals in the dormant cells, which would damage plant tissue much the way they damage human tissue. Being able to halt photosynthesis is one of the most important adaptations in evergreen plants, ensuring their survival during the winter months.

The woods of Vermont and New Hampshire are home to three common evergreen ferns, which can be told apart by examining the shape of the leaves. The aptly named Christmas fern (*Polystichum acrostichoides*) is the most common, with fronds up to 2 feet tall and leaves that are so-called "singly cut": they grow directly from the stem and have no notches in them. The marginal woodfern (*Dryopteris marginalis*) is of similar size but has doubly cut leaves: each leaf is deeply notched so that it appears at first glance to be a compound leaf. Finally there is the smaller spinulose woodfern (*Dryopteris spinulos*), whose fronds average only 12 inches in length and whose leaves are triply cut: the notches on the leaves are themselves notched, giving the appearance of compound leaves growing from compound leaves.

Even in the harsh midwinter months, there are green plants to be found in our local woods. Being graced with the sight of one makes winter much easier to bear. ∾

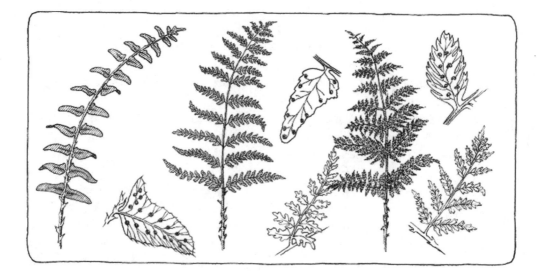

There's a New Bird at Your Feeder

~

Anne Margolis

Birders who have been keeping a tally of their feeder visitors over the past half-century may have noticed an unusual trend: some species that once strictly summered here, including tufted titmice, northern cardinals, mourning doves, and evening grosbeaks, are now spending more if not all of their winters here, too.

According to Kent McFarland of the Vermont Institute of Natural Science (VINS), these proverbial "canaries in the coal mine" are expanding their winter ranges northward because of changes in food, habitat, and climate.

In the first Vermont Breeding Bird Atlas (BBA), published in 1985, for example, there were just a handful of tufted titmouse accounts in winter in the Connecticut River valley. "Maybe northern Windsor County was the farthest northern record," McFarland says. The revision of the Vermont BBA, soon to be published, now includes winter records of the tufted titmouse all over the state.

Cardinals, now somewhat regular visitors to our region's feeders in winter, were also once rare, says McFarland. New studies indicate that the cardinal depends on stored fat to survive in cold climates, and that winter tem-

peratures are thus the limiting factor in determining its northern range limits.

Similar observations in the United Kingdom led to a study in which researchers discovered that from 1970 to 1990 the northern range boundaries of what were considered to be southerly species shifted northward by 19 kilometers, on average.

There are three schools of thought on why this range expansion is happening. First, more people are feeding birds in winter, and the birds are following the feeders. It is estimated that a third of households in North America each distribute 60 pounds of bird food every year. "Birds can hang out if they have the food supply," says McFarland.

Another explanation is habitat change, which benefits some species while harming others. One example is the wild turkey, whose range has significantly increased because of successful management and the increased availability of the mixed habitat it likes.

Of greater concern is our warming climate. "Birds shift ranges according to availability of habitat, whether it be in the form of food resources, nesting habitat, or decreases in competition with similar species, within physiological limits," says Rosalind Renfrew, director of the Vermont BBA project at VINS. "Climate change can affect all of these factors."

Bolstering the warming theory is increased evidence of migratory birds coming north and laying eggs earlier than before. A recent analysis of the Cornell Nest Record Program, which includes hundreds of thousands of nest records from the past 50 years, found that red-winged blackbirds and bluebirds have significantly earlier egg-laying times than they did a half-century ago, a change attributed to warming temperatures over the same period of time.

A report by the Climate Change Research Center at the University of New Hampshire found that, "Over the past 100 years, and especially the last 30 years, all of the climate change indicators for the region reveal a warming trend." The average annual temperature of the Northeast, according to the report, has increased 1.8°F since 1899, 1.4°F of that warming happening in the past 30 years. Winter temperatures have increased more than temperatures in any other season—an impressive average of 4.4°F over the past 30 years.

A 1988 study showed that range boundaries of 50 songbirds are dictated by average minimum January temperatures, and ongoing research shows that some of these species' ranges have significantly shifted in direct relationship to the warming climate.

Some bird species will benefit from a warming climate, while others will decline. According to a recent Forest Service/University of Maine study, more than half of all birds in the East will decline as a result of climate change, while 20 percent will increase because of changes in available habitat. The same study predicts the

ranges occupied by about 40 percent of bird species will decrease, while those of about 20 percent will increase.

With shifting ranges, too, comes a whole series of shifting relationships between bird species once separated geographically. Diseases may spread, such as the conjunctivitis carried by non-native house finches that can infect other birds, including siskins and goldfinches. Competition for nesting sites may also occur, such as that between cavity nesters like the chickadee, a common winter resident, and the tufted titmouse, newly on the scene.

"Nobody has looked at interspecific conflicts yet," says McFarland, but he's quick to add that it's most important to look at new species arrivals as an indicator that something is going on in the greater ecosystem. "Maybe a few birds are not a big deal," he says. "However, there may be all kinds of cascading effects in the ecosystem we don't know about yet. They are warning flags that tell us, whoa, there are some changes going on in our environment." ∾

February

FIRST WEEK

1

The familiar bird's-nest-shaped seed heads of Queen
Anne's lace contain emergency food for birds.

Most mammals sit tight during a snowstorm,
tucked in their dens, warm and dry. Wait two
days and the woods will be full of their tracks.

Time to bring pussy willow shoots
indoors for a preview of spring.

The tapering shape of balsam firs allows them
to shed snow when the load gets too heavy.

In the depths of winter, the temperature in a beaver
lodge may average 60°F warmer than outdoors.

SECOND WEEK

2

Raccoons go wandering on the warmer nights and
may not end up in the den they started from.

Blue jays may be cleaning out your feeder,
but they are sharp lookouts and will sound
the alarm if any danger is sighted.

On warm days, look for stoneflies
perched on rocks near clean rivers
and streams. They will mate, and the
female will lay eggs back in the water.

Deep snow makes life difficult for fox and
deer, but it allows the snowshoe hare to
reach a new supply of tender shoots.

THIRD WEEK

3

Acrobatic aerial courtship displays by ravens are under way. Rolling, tumbling, and soaring are accompanied by the loud territorial call, a resonating *quork*.

Maple sugar makers are on alert. Sap will start flowing in earnest anytime now.

On warm days, snow fleas climb from the ground to the surface of the snow along tree trunks. They look like a sprinkling of pepper—except that they hop.

Single male pileated woodpeckers drum frequently. Their loud drumming diminishes at the end.

FOURTH WEEK

4

If a muskrat's food supply is used up, it will emerge from the safety of its burrow to search for grassy areas bare of snow.

It's time to clean out birdhouses, except those being used by flying squirrels.

Chickadee flocks are breaking up; listen for the two-note territorial whistle of the male— *feebee*—the first note higher than the second.

Wild turkeys seem to get braver as food supplies dwindle. They may venture into yards and orchards for spilled birdseed and fallen fruit.

The Bobcat's Snow Day

Dan Lambert

Snow day! The announcement draws squeals of joy from students throughout the school district and groans from parents who must scramble to provide care for their kids and face a treacherous commute. But fourth-graders with overdue homework and harried parents aren't the only ones whose fortunes hang in the balance when new snow blankets the region. A snowfall can bring salvation or suffering to wild critters as well.

Take the bobcat, for example. This surprisingly small carnivore stands little more than housecat-high on small paws that sink in fluffy snow. The bobcat cannot afford the energetic cost of swimming through deep powder, so its movements are limited to windswept rises, protruding rocks or logs, or trails packed down by other wildlife. Long, hungry hours are spent confined to the shelter of caves or upturned stumps when the snow piles high. A mere six inches of fluff can restrict bobcat movement, so it's easy to see why they approach their distributional limit here in northern New England.

Bobcats mate in late winter, with a two-month gestation period leading to birth in early spring. The demands of motherhood during this period require that females maintain a healthy diet despite the challenges of a snowy world. Unfortunately, the bobcat's meat-only menu features few selections, most of which gain an advantage from a fresh snowfall.

One entrée helped by a snow day is ruffed grouse, who sprout comb-like projections on their feet each fall, doubling the surface area of their feet and easing snow-top travel. When the temperature drops, they burrow beneath the insulating snow and roost in cavities that can be 50° warmer than the ambient temperature on a frigid night. If the snow is soft powder, they may simply dive into their subnivean roosts, which provide concealment from predators as well as warmth. Upon emergence, grouse can forage on aspen, oak, and beech buds on branches higher up in the trees, thanks to the boost from the fresh snow.

Deeper snow also provides another bobcat staple, the snowshoe hare, with access to a new food supply. Hares are masters of energy conservation, occupying a small home range in winter and hopping beyond their comfort zone only when pressed to locate new buds and twigs. New snow means new food, all without leaving the comforts of home. When not seeking food, hares hunker down in sheltered depressions beneath the snow-laden branches of conifer saplings. Outside these "forms," snowshoe hares pack down a network of runways with their extraordinary hind feet, all the while camouflaged in their winter-white coats.

Although they lack the hare's large feet and cryptic coloration, white-tailed deer share the hare's affinity for shelter among conifers. While deeper snow doesn't benefit deer, they adapt to it by yarding up in large softwood stands, tramping down their own trail network in the shadow of hemlocks, northern white cedars, red spruce, balsam fir, or white pine. Once these trees reach a sufficient height, they form canopies that intercept snow and provide refuge from chilling winds. However, a trade-off occurs when snow conditions permit bobcats to stalk a known yard for bedding deer. A stealthy tom can pounce on the back of the much larger mammal and administer a fatal bite to the back of the neck.

The smaller female bobcats are less capable of such feats and rely more heavily on small prey, such as voles and mice. Yet rodents, too, escape bobcat jaws in their tunnels. They may be safe from bobcats beneath the snow, but they face a persistent threat from weasels and remain subject to the capricious winter climate. After the storm passes and the snowpack begins to age, the tables turn again.

As snow ages, hidden cavities begin to chill, since old snow insulates only one-eighth as well as fresh snow. Sudden thaws can flood subnivean runways, drowning small mammals or flushing them to the surface. An ice storm can trap carbon dioxide in tunnel systems and present an air-quality haz-

ard to voles and mice. Just as the fortunes of rodents decline, the prospects for bobcats brighten. Hardened crust enables easier access to deer immobilized in their yards, to hunting perches overlooking snowshoe runways, and to grouse unable to burrow for refuge.

The balance between predator and prey shifts as each snowstorm brings relief to some animals and deprivation to others. And while a snow day can provide a welcome change to schoolchildren, it can also tip the balance of life and death between predator and prey. ∾

Deer in Tough Winters

Chuck Wooster

Few of us think about deer at this time of year. There are no fawns to be fawned over, no legal season for hunting, and only rare roadside sightings. Yet for the deer themselves, late winter is the season of desperation.

The whitetail's strategy for surviving winter is, quite simply, to wait it out. While other animals flee southward, or hibernate in holes, or even freeze solidly (the wood frog), whitetails hunker down and hope for the best.

Which, in winters with heavy snows that linger, isn't very good. What happens to deer under these circumstances? Author Richard Nelson puts it this way in his book, *Heart and Blood: Living With Deer in America*: "Imagine that 90 percent of our houses became unusable during the coldest and most stressful months, forcing us to crowd into the remaining 10 percent. And to make matters worse, 90 percent of the grocery stores were closed because of snow and other factors, so all of us had to survive on 10 percent of the normal food supply. This is the predicament northern deer face each year."

The survival strategy of the deer herd includes the certainty that some individuals will starve to death and the hope that not every one will do so. In an open winter, one with little snow cover, the gamble pays off handsomely: fewer than 5 percent of the individuals may die. But in a severe winter, the odds are less favorable: 30 to 50 percent or more of the animals may die in some areas.

The crucial factor for whitetail survival is the 10 percent of the "houses" that remain usable all winter—the specialized habitat known to biologists (and other deer aficionados) as deeryards. Writing in *Northern Woodlands* magazine, Stephen Long describes a deeryard as "a thick stand of softwood that is tall enough—at least 35 feet tall—to form a good overhead canopy that provides shelter from the snow and cold. The canopy intercepts snow, which hangs up on branches until it evaporates. The density of the stand creates a barrier to wind, so that the wind-chill factor is less brutal inside than out. In addition, the snow-laden boughs serve almost as a blanket, restricting heat loss into the atmosphere and creating a pocket of warmth for a bedded deer. Within the shelter of a deeryard is a microclimate that is measurably warmer, less windy, and has considerably less snow."

The availability of deeryard habitat—not the amount of hunting and predation—is the limiting factor that determines the viability of the deer herd. State wildlife officials, who are entrusted by law with the management of all wild animals, have special land-use designations to help protect the most important deeryards. Local land trusts also help steer human development away from crucial habitat. In general, biologists believe that a deeryard needs to have a minimum of between 50 and 100 acres to be effective in the harshest winters, with roughly three-quarters of the forest cover in mature softwood and the rest in young hardwood and softwood that provide winter browse.

At this time of year, finding deer (or the frozen impressions in the snow where they have bedded down) is a sure-fire indication that you've stumbled across a deeryard. Which, if you sympathize at all with the plight of deer, you should avoid doing. If you know where your local deer are yarded up, consider choosing some other place for your late winter outings. Why force deer to expend precious energy fleeing from you when there are so many other places available for recreation?

And if you happen upon a deeryard accidentally, the best bet is simply to turn around and retrace your steps rather than proceeding ahead and further pushing the deer.

Finally, our beloved dogs pose one of the greatest dangers to deer at this time of year, particularly when there is a crust over the snow that supports wide, soft dog pads but not narrow, sharp, whitetail hooves. Canines by nature love to chase deer. A half-starved coyote chasing a half-starved deer with both animals' lives at stake is one thing; Fido out for a romp after dinner is something else altogether.

So, keep your dog close to home, yourself out of the deeryards and, most of all, keep the deer in your thoughts as they go through their most brutal season. Before you know it, we'll soon be catching sight of fawns at the edges of fields all across Vermont and New Hampshire. ❧

Dead Birds Don't Fly

Ted Levin

I see him high above the Wilder Dam, which spans the Connecticut River between Lebanon, New Hampshire, and Hartford, Vermont. With wings flat and primary flight feathers extended, he circles the edge of a thermal, head and tail white, body and wings brown. Around and around he flies, with eyes keen enough to take in the whole Upper Valley.

I no longer think of the open water below Wilder Dam as just another riverine attraction for wintering ducks. The arrival of the bald eagle changed all that. I first saw the big bird in December of 1981. The eagle, an immature bird, stayed for a few days and then vanished. Each year since, one or two bald eagles have returned to the Upper Valley for the winter. But our neighborhood was once not so hospitable; bald eagles were missing from the Upper Valley for nearly four decades.

By the late 1940s, wintering bald eagles had mysteriously disappeared from this stretch of the Connecticut River and from most of the United States. Use of the synthetic compound DDT (dichloro-diphenyl-trichloroethane) had increased dramatically after World War II to combat everything from mosquitoes to head lice, and researchers in the upper Mid-

west were convinced that DDT was causing problems for the eagles. Data from their studies confirmed that the dead and dying birds they were studying—robins, marsh hawks, and eagles—had large concentrations of DDT in their fat and brains. The smaller birds died outright from the chemical while the larger birds laid eggs with thin shells that broke under the weight of the incubating parent.

But was there evidence from the Northeast? Beginning in 1960, Betty Sherrard, an energetic naturalist, had fretted over the robins that convulsed and died each spring on her lawn in Hanover, New Hampshire. In 1962, she read Rachel Carson's *Silent Spring* and suspected that DDT was to blame; every April, Dartmouth College, in Hanover, sprayed its beloved elm trees with DDT to try to control the spread of Dutch elm disease. Sherrard asked two Dartmouth College biochemists, Drs. Charles and Doris Wurster, to investigate the situation.

They agreed to help. For several days in April 1963, approximately 1,300 pounds of DDT were sprayed on more than 1,000 elms on the Dartmouth campus. Just across the river, the town of Norwich, Vermont, was not spraying their elms. The Wursters thus had the perfect setup for a scientific experiment: a control population of birds free from DDT just across the river from the affected population in Hanover.

The Wursters and two friends surveyed a 15-acre section of Hanover and an ecologically similar section of Norwich. They counted robins on their way to work, at lunch, and on their daily rounds between April 8 and mid-May. After mid-May, the counts were spaced at intervals of two and three days until mid-June. The results were stunning.

Nothing appeared to happen the morning after spraying the elms; the DDT took weeks to travel from the elms into the soil and into the earthworms. By mid-May, however, dead robins began to appear in Hanover, and all the casualties were found to have high levels of DDT in their tissues. Although Norwich had a few dead robins here and there, none had high levels of DDT.

The Hanover study area lost more than 70 percent of its breeding robins in 1963. Norwich's study area, relatively free from the effects of the chemical, actually gained a few birds that year.

Not everyone was convinced by the results of the study. One California scientist claimed that the robins had simply flown across the river, thereby explaining the population decline in Hanover and the slight rise in Norwich. But dead birds don't fly. Fortunately, the ground crew at Dartmouth heeded the Wursters' warning and switched to a less-toxic compound, methoxychlor, in 1964. Although a few robins died that spring, the re-sult perhaps of residual DDT, the population rebounded, and there was no evidence of the chemical in other species of birds.

Across North America, populations of bald eagles (as well as osprey, peregrine falcons, and brown pelicans) have staged a remarkable comeback. Today, several thousand pairs of eagles nest in the lower 48 states, many at sites that had been abandoned for decades. Ever since 1988, along the shore of Lake Umbagog in northern New Hampshire, a pair has built their nest in the same towering white pine that had stood empty of eagles since 1949.

There are three eagles at Wilder Dam this winter of 2003. For that, we all owe a big thanks to the local researchers and naturalists who came to the eagles' aid forty years ago this spring. ∽

Winter's Bug Season

Bill Amos

In one form or another—eggs, larvae, pupae, nymphs, adults—insects are as much with us when it's below zero as they are in July. Some, tucked away, become inactive before the first frost; others gather in metabolically warmed colonies or exist in a transitional stage.

One insect, however, the winter stonefly, finds an upland stream's frigidity as acceptable in January as in summer. This intrepid insect crawls out of the water onto an exposed rock at midday in midwinter, its dark body absorbing the sun's warmth to raise metabolism necessary for shucking its nymphal skin. It briefly takes wing, mates, and completes its life cycle, all in the course of a few short days.

Now is the time of year to be on the lookout for these unusual insects. Emergence begins in January, reaches a peak in February, and tapers off in March, the schedule determined and timed by increasing day length and an almost imperceptible rise in water temperature. An adult winter stonefly is about an inch in length, has long, overlapping wings folded flat on its back, and has a dark, flattened body. A pair of antennae faces forward, and a matched set of short tail filaments, called cerci, extends off the back.

For most of the year, winter stoneflies (also called boreal willowflies, *Taeniopteryx nivalis*) live in brooks in their nymphal stage, undergoing as many as 30 molts per year. In the partly frozen brook near my house, these sturdy nymphs clamber over stones and under rocks all winter, actively foraging for food. Stonefly nymphs have strong, biting mouth parts, and this winter species is mainly carnivorous, scurrying around after midge larvae and mayfly nymphs, though, if these aren't plentiful, algae and plant fragments will do.

Single, fingerlike gills protrude from the winter stonefly nymph's underside at the bases of its legs. The gills are quite small compared to the size of the insect's body, meaning that winter stoneflies can only live in clean, highly aerated water. Their presence in large numbers indicates that a brook is healthy and relatively pollution-free.

Though there are some 400 different North American stonefly species, only 22 are found in Vermont and New Hampshire, and only two species hatch at this time of year. Any stonefly nymph can be recognized by its two long, straight tail filaments and flattened body and is easily distinguished from similar mayfly nymphs, which have three wide tail filaments.

In the water, a stonefly nymph's outstretched legs reach out onto a rock surface like grappling hooks, each leg ending in a large, two-clawed foot. The legs themselves are flattened and held against the rock to offer as little resistance to the current as possible. The insect's head and long body also present a very low profile, allowing the stonefly nymph to scuttle like a crab in the rock/water interface, where friction retards the current. The nymph never rises on tiptoe, for to do so would mean being plucked off and whirled downstream.

When the full-grown nymph crawls out of the icy brook to shed its nymphal skin, a split appears down the middle of its back, and the body swells as air in its tracheal tubes inflates inner tissues. Holding on to the rock with its front feet, the emerging adult withdraws its long tail filaments from their thin sheaths, then the legs from theirs. The wings, previously existing only as pads on the nymph, are now exposed and begin to expand and harden in the wintry air. As the adult appears, it leaves behind the lining to major tracheal tubes and part of its gut, which remain attached to the rock along with the shed exoskeleton.

Once it's time to fly, the winter stonefly takes wing slowly and awkwardly, alighting on bare bushes and tree trunks near the stream bank. Stoneflies tend not to fly much and, if disturbed, may scurry off instead. By midday, however, large numbers of dark adults will be fluttering short distances in preparation for mating.

The insects engage in courtship duets, males drumming their bodies against the surface they're on, females responding with a drummed "I am here." Mating soon follows.

The following day, females fly heavily back to the brook and drop large packets of eggs into the water. The eggs swell, separate, and are swirled by the current until they become caught under stones. Mortality is extremely high: a single female lays several thousand eggs, and though there are many females at work, barely enough young survive to ensure continuation of the species.

Winter being winter, the adult winter stoneflies don't last much longer and never make it far from their nymphal brook home. They may nibble in desultory fashion on blue-green cyanophytes growing on tree bark, but they soon succumb to the cold, their work and lives complete. ∾

Are Worms Really Our Friends?

~

Alan Parker

What was it we learned about earthworms? When we were kids, they were squiggly things that either fascinated or disgusted us. If we fished, they were likely the key to our first angling success. As we made our way into the garden, we came to call them "nature's little farmers," tilling and fertilizing in one operation. Charles Darwin described their beneficial effect on soil structure and fertility. Aristotle referred to them as "the intestines of the Earth."

Forest scientists, however, are now asking that we rethink how beneficial earthworms really are to the natural processes at work in forest soils. They may be doing more harm than good.

The common night crawler we all know (*Lumbricus terrestris*) is one of many species of earthworms, all members of the phylum Annelida, which also includes worms and leeches. Whatever earthworms were native to North America found themselves scraped into oblivion by the last Ice Age; only remnants of certain species remained in the southeast and on the Pacific coast. Until, that is, European settlers came, bringing European earthworms in soil, plant roots, and livestock hooves.

Fast forward to the 1980s, when forest ecologists noted a decline in the quantity and health of understory shrubs and wildflowers in the northern forests of the United States and in Canada. Research in Minnesota, Wisconsin, and Ontario first focused on the possible presence of toxic minerals like lead and mercury. Testing for these elements came up empty, but scientists noticed that areas most subject to this decline contained more earthworms than did places less affected.

Further study showed that earthworms are most common around forest lakes, ponds, and streams, in part because of anglers' common practice of depositing unused fishing bait there.

Farmers and gardeners appreciate earthworms in agricultural soils because they digest coarse organic matter and turn it into "castings" that are high in vital plant nutrients and because their tunnels loosen and aerate compacted dirt, which improves drainage. When ample water and nutrients are available, as happens with intensive agriculture, enhanced drainage is beneficial to crop growth.

In the forest, however, the carpet of decaying organic matter that covers the forest floor is essential to nutrient conservation. From top to bottom, this mat ranges from newly fallen leaves and woody material to more decayed matter, called duff. Just like a sponge, this organic matter retains water and is home to a complex web of microlife that slowly processes nutrients, feeding both the plants and the microlife itself.

Worms introduced into this web act like a garbage disposal. In the presence of large numbers of worms, the duff layer that normally takes several years to decay can be almost fully digested in one summer. The result is a nearly bare, more mineralized soil that becomes foreign ground to many native forest plant species like large-flowered trilliums, yellow violets, and Solomon's seal. The rare goblin fern, for example, native to some northern hardwood forests, hosts a fungus that assists the fern in extracting soil nutrients. When earthworms graze the fungus, the fern loses a vital advantage and may thus be nudged toward extinction.

The problem is greatest in hardwood forests having neutral to alkaline soils, which earthworms prefer over the more acidic soils typically found beneath softwood.

One damaging result of earthworm activity is that affected soils become more receptive to other invasive species. In southern Vermont and New Hampshire, landowners are noticing that the understory in oak- and maple-dominated forests is becoming overrun with species like buckthorn and barberry. Absent the natural conditions favoring regeneration of native species, these invaders threaten not just natural wildflowers and shrubs but also the birds and other animals that rely on them for food and cover. The invaders threaten the very future of these forests as productive timber resources: buckthorn makes lousy hardwood flooring.

Scientists, often cursed with the task of giving us new things to worry about, don't foresee any way to remove invading worms from places already colonized. Some do, however, believe that the spread of non-native earthworms could be slowed, especially if more people were aware of the problem. Anglers should not leave worms behind when their creel is full, and people in some areas may need to consider restrictions on worms as bait. In addition, landowners can be attentive to symptoms of the problem and can find sources of native plant seed stock to recolonize affected areas.

Worms don't migrate quickly; they advance no more than 15–30 feet per year. (That's part of the reason why the problem is only coming to light now, hundreds of years after the first European earthworms arrived.) Perhaps common sense and care will keep them in the garden, where their virtues can best be appreciated. ✑

Spring Flush

Geoff Wilson

Most northeasterners are familiar with the causes of acid rain: nitrates and sulfates from the burning of fossil fuels that enter the atmosphere and cause rain, snow, and fog to be more acidic than they would otherwise be. Most people probably also know that acid rain can kill fish; it has been known for over a decade that the higher the acidity of a given lake or stream, the lower the number of fish species that will be found in it.

But what few people know is that springtime is when the problem is most acute. The reason is very straightforward: acidity that has been held up in the snowpack all winter is released into streams very quickly during the spring thaw. The resulting surge brings streams and rivers to their most acidic levels of the year.

Some streams are affected by this surge more than others. Indeed, although acid precipitation has been falling on the Northeast for decades, some streams still support high species diversity while others do not. The majority of northeastern streams fall somewhere in between—not, on average, overly acidic, yet still susceptible to the high pulse of acidification that occurs during the spring

thaw. Understanding what is happening in these streams is of utmost importance since any benefits from reduced air pollution and acid rain will first be seen in the recovery of these streams.

How much a particular stream is affected by acidification depends on two key properties of the soils in the surrounding watershed. The first is how well the soil drains or, more technically, the residence time of water in the soil. Acidity needs time in contact with individual soil particles to be neutralized, just as in a good cup of coffee, water needs time in contact with the coffee grounds to absorb the most flavor. During snowmelt and heavy rainstorms, water moves through the soil so quickly that this neutralization never has a chance to happen.

The second key property of soil is called buffering capacity—the soil's ability to neutralize acidity if given the time to do so. Soils rich in calcium and other positively charged ions are able to exchange these ions for the positively charged hydrogen ions that make rainwater acidic. Soils with good buffering capacity have lots of these positively charged ions; soils with poor buffering capacity do not.

Farmers and gardeners, incidentally, spread lime to increase the buffering capacity of their soils, knowing that the calcium in lime is an excellent way to counteract the effects of acid rain. Natural soil buffering capacity, on the other hand, is rebuilt very slowly by the weathering of calcium and other positively charged ions from the bedrock beneath the soil.

When poorly buffered soils are unable to counteract the acidity, aluminum and other metals are leached out of the soil and into streams and rivers. In high concentrations, these metals become poisonous to trout and other aquatic life.

In our region, the Battenkill River in western Vermont drains an area underlain by marble bedrock. Marble is a rock rich in calcium, and consequently the Battenkill is a good example of a stream with very well buffered soils. Not coincidentally, it has also historically been a very good trout stream. In contrast, Hubbard Brook in the western White Mountains drains an area underlain by granitic rock relatively poor in calcium. These soils have a limited buffering capacity, and though the stream is not normally very acidic, it is very susceptible to acidification during the spring runoff. In fact, the water in this brook can be 100-times more acidic during spring runoff than during late summer when the flow is at its lowest.

Our problem in the Northeast is that our soils are being depleted by acid rain faster than they are being replenished by the bedrock. This has been true for the past half century, and many of our soils now have very little buffering capacity left. Recent improvements in air quality have led to a slight decrease in the acidity of precipitation falling in the

Northeast, and while this is a step in the right direction, it has done nothing except slow the rate at which damage is occurring. Until the rate of replenishment is higher than the rate of removal—until acid rain from the combustion of fossil fuels ceases to bathe the Northeast—our soils will continue to lose their ability to mitigate the effects of acid precipitation, and the spring thaw will become ever more stressful for fish and other aquatic life. ∾

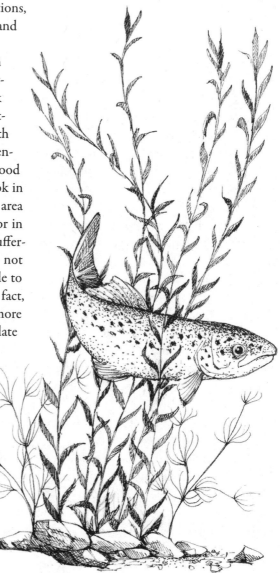

March

FIRST WEEK

The dog begins to shed.

Pussy willow roots are in ditches in
wetlands, and the shrub responds to
the very first signs of thawing.

Most great horned owls begin nesting. Some
may have started over a month ago.

Pine grosbeaks and cedar waxwings
come to town to feast on crabapples.

Saw-whet owls may be calling a monotonic
too, too, too, too, too, repeated endlessly.

Red-winged blackbirds and other early
migrants stay close to the sumac patch, eating
berries, especially during bad weather.

SECOND WEEK

The robin's *cherriup cheerily* signifies that spring is here.

Skunks roll out of their dens and
embark on a long prowl. Six to eight
young are born two months later.

Mourning cloak butterflies overwinter as
adults and can be seen flying on warm days.

Black bears emerge from hibernation having
lost as much as 40 percent of their body weight.

Melting snow may reveal small fruit trees
that have been girdled. Though many different
rodents do this, the meadow vole is a prime suspect.

THIRD WEEK

Crows are building new nests. The old ones may
have been taken over by great horned owls.

Foxes give birth. They will be weaned
in about nine weeks but will stay with
their mother through the summer.

Wood frogs are usually the first frogs to
appear. On half-melted ponds, they may
gather at the edge of the ice, where they
look like sunbathers on a white beach.

When the snow melts, don't blame shrews
for those tunnels in the lawn. They do live
there, but the tunnels were made by moles.

FOURTH WEEK

A litter of two to four baby northern flying
squirrels is born. Southern flying squirrels will
give birth a couple of weeks from now.

Eager Canada geese are pressing northward,
seeming to fly faster now than in the fall.

Listen for the nasal *peents* of woodcocks rising
from wet meadows. Their twilight songs will
continue for the next four or five weeks.

Wood frogs are arriving at ponds to breed.
Egg laying is synchronized, and adults will
return to the woods within a week or two.

Litter Bugs

Alan Pistorius

Given an estimated around-the-globe average of 100,000 per cubic meter of soil, it seems astonishing that springtails (the tiny creatures often called "snowfleas") are frequently overlooked. Spotty distribution isn't to blame for their invisibility. They occur in woodland and in grassland, in deserts and on permanent Arctic snowfields, in caves and greenhouses, even on fresh and salt water. Nor are populations thin. One study in Denmark concluded that 16 million individuals of a single species inhabited a one-acre forest plot.

We go about our outdoor business blithely unaware of springtails because they are tiny, silent, and live for the most part hidden in duff and leaf litter and in the top inch or so of loose soil. Most species are dark of hue—black, gray, dark blue—which is why casual encounters hereabouts are likely to occur on warmish winter or early spring days when springtails are active on the snow surface, where they appear to wide-eyed first-time observers as animated pepper grains.

But what exactly is a springtail? Your natural history handbook or insect field guide probably identifies springtails as a primitive order of insects. But specialists in the field are now largely agreed that springtails aren't insects at all but rather organisms forming an order—even a class—of their own. They do share characteristics with insects—most notably three body parts and six legs—but they differ from them in important regards. For example, their mouthparts—external in insects—are enclosed in the head. And unlike insects, typical springtails absorb oxygen directly through the soft cuticle, and feature either small patches of simple eyes (which provide poor vision) or no eyes at all.

With the aid of magnification, one can see toward the rear of a springtail the celebrated action feature, the "furca" or "furcula." This two-prong-tipped organ is normally held forward against the underbody, secured by a catch called the "tenaculum." When alarmed (or merely traveling), the springtail releases the catch, and the tensed furca drives down and back into the ground (or log or leaf or snow or water), catapulting its owner up and away, antennae over tea kettle. We are likely to notice these minuscule soft-bodied creatures only en masse. When an assemblage has detected your presence, they will begin to jump, and because the human eye can't follow them in flight, the pool of organisms will seem simply to evaporate. It is, as far as I know, the only demonstration in nature of the reverse of spontaneous generation.

Taken as a group, springtails consume a remarkably varied diet. A few are predatory, hunting down tardigrades, nematodes, rotifers, even other springtails. Some cave-dwelling species may live entirely on soil bacteria, while those roaming the surface of stagnant pools are probably grazing on algae. Certain highly specialized springtails live their entire lives on cleanup patrol in ant or termite nests, where they are thought to subsist on bits of food dropped or regurgitated by their hosts. Species that periodically or permanently occupy snow or ice fields are assumed to glean wind-blown pollen grains and spores. Many species eat frass (arthropod droppings), while fungi and plant material, both fresh and decayed, are standard food for the majority of species.

Typical insects rely on copulation to initiate the critical business of reproduction. Lacking external genitalia, springtails employ a fastidiously impersonal method. A male secretes a viscous material, which—by raising his posterior—is drawn up to form a stalk, on top of which he deposits a spherical packet of sperm. This structure, which looks, microscopically, like a golf ball perched on a long and very thin tee, is called a spermatophore, and males produce a number of them during periodic reproductive phases. If a receptive female of the appropriate species happens   p e n s by, she takes the sperm packet up through her genital slit. Liquids inside her body cause the packet tissue to swell and burst, releasing the sperm for egg-fertilization duty.

If this system for combining precious genetic material seems to us haphazard, it apparently strikes a few springtails that way as well. Males of certain species build a fence of spermatophores around a likely female, a strategy presumably designed to ensure reproductive success by prompting the "eenie-meenie-miney-moe" response. Males of a few species even drag females to their spermatophores. Clearly, however, earth's environments are yearly strewn with quadrillions of what are destined to be leftover springtail spermatophores. Nothing is wasted in nature, of course, and many of these end up as minute contributions to soil fertility. But others serve springtails more directly. Encountering intact sperm packets—particularly those teed up by other species—foraging males are likely to eat them. ✍

There's Something in the Soil

Chuck Wooster

Everybody knows that New Hampshire and Vermont are different. But few know just how dissimilar the so-called twin states are—they're different right down to the core. Cross the river and the soil's different, the bedrock's different, and these differences have greatly affected the human landscapes of the two states.

A story making the rounds is that Vermont came from North America while New Hampshire came from Africa. While evocative, this isn't true. The bedrock of both states was formed side by side under the ocean off North America and then thrust above the waves by a collision between North America, Europe, and Africa. The crucial difference between the two states' geology, however, is that Vermont is closer to the center of North America while New Hampshire is closer to the edge. This may seem overly obvious, but it has led to three significant consequences.

The first is in the composition of the bedrock itself. The entire region was underwater when the rocks of the two states were being formed—the coast was where the Adirondacks are now. Vermont, under shallow coastal water teeming with marine life, was covered by sediments rich in lime. New Hampshire, farther out to sea, was under water too deep for the formation of lime. Nearly 50 percent of Vermont's bedrock is naturally rich in limy minerals. In New Hampshire, the percentage is only 5 percent.

If the continental collision had been a head-on car crash, Vermont would have been the trunk of the car and New Hampshire the hood. So the second consequence of location is that a sizable percentage of New Hampshire's rocks were smashed so much that they melted together and were recast as new, crystalline rocks: the granites of the Granite State. Just under 50% of New Hampshire is underlain by crystalline rock. In Vermont, by contrast, the figure is only about 20%. Crystalline rocks erode into gravelly soils, and gravelly soils tend to be acidic because water runs right through them and washes out the soluble, acid-resistant minerals.

Third, immediately after the Ice Age, 40 percent of Vermont was underwater compared with only about 15 percent of New Hampshire. (Both states are less than 4 percent underwater today.) This flooding occurred because the ice sheets covering New England were heavy enough to depress the earth's crust—by nearly 500 feet in northwest Vermont, closer to the center of continental glaciation, by 200 feet at Lebanon/White River, but scarcely at all by the New Hampshire seacoast. The soils from flooded land are rich in fine-grained clays and silts, and these soils hold moisture better, are less acidic, and are more fertile than unflooded soils.

As for those folks who believe that geological differences can be felt immediately upon crossing the Connecticut River, well, they can. The Ammonoosuc fault runs just along the Vermont bank of the Connecticut through the Upper Valley. During the continental collision, a significant chunk of bedrock was thrust up and eroded away along this fault. The result? The differing rocks of Vermont and New Hampshire are now found cheek by jowl, right along the Connecticut River, rather than slowly transitioning over many miles.

So how do these geologic differences affect the human landscape of the two states? These days not much, because fossil fuels influence our local economies far more than local resources. But for most of the two states' histories, these geologic differences have made a major difference, primarily in the distribution and prominence of agriculture. In 1900, Vermont's economy was among the most agriculturally based of any of the 50 states while New Hampshire's was among the least.

Take the mid-1800s, for example, when wool was selling at $70 per pound (in today's dollars) and agriculture was far and away the most profitable use of land in either state. Northern New England was home to 3 million sheep, nearly two-thirds of which were in Vermont. Nineteenth-century wool production was entirely dependent on natural soil fertility, not on added fertilizers. In 1860, Vermont's farmers clipped an average of 6.1 pounds of wool per animal compared

with New Hampshire's 5.0 pounds. Not only were there far more sheep in Vermont but also these sheep were producing 20% more wool than their counterparts in New Hampshire. All because of the soil.

But New Hampshire's acidic soils were not entirely without economic potential. The sandy soils of the New Hampshire seacoast are ideally suited for growing red oak, white oak, and white pine—three tree species that together are among the world's best for building wooden ships. While Vermonters were raising Merino sheep, New Hampshire's coastal residents were world-renowned shipbuilders.

That agriculture has historically mattered far more to Vermont's economy than to New Hampshire's, however, is not entirely due to differences in soil quality. It is also due to another natural resource: New Hampshire's abundance of hydropower. But that's another story. ∾

Limy   Acidic

Acid Rain Falls Unevenly

Virginia Barlow

In recent years, red spruce decline, sugar maple dieback, and other signs of trouble in the forest have all been attributed to acid deposition, which reaches the forest in rain, snow, fog, and dust. Studies of individual trees in small areas have tended to confirm this link, but measurements of the effects of pollution over a wide area have been difficult to come by. Just what are the consequences of the shower of acidifying sulfur and nitrogen from coal-burning power plants, cars, and other sources on our forests overall?

In order to get a handle on this, the governors of the New England states and the premiers of the eastern Canadian provinces have jointly established the Forest Mapping Group (FMG), a large group of scientists charged with determining how bad the damage really is and calculating what changes will be needed to keep eastern forests productive and healthy. In September of 2003, the FMG released a preliminary report, which examines Vermont and Newfoundland in detail. The findings are very disturbing: one-third of the forestland in Vermont is currently at risk of being seriously damaged—possibly irreparably—by acid deposition.

How did the FMG make this determination? Scientists combined data on atmospheric sulfur and nitrogen deposition, and bedrock and surficial geology, with data from state and federal surveys of tree-harvesting rates, statewide maps of soils, and models that analyze soil chemistry and forest tree composition to determine two crucial indices: the critical load index and the deposition index.

The critical load is simply the amount of sulfur and nitrogen that can rain down on a particular section of forest without stripping plant-essential nutrients from the soil. Since some soils are naturally able to resist acid deposition better than others, the critical index varies widely across Vermont, with much of the forest along the Green Mountain spine being the most susceptible and the forest of the Connecticut River valley being the least susceptible.

The second crucial factor, the deposition index, compares the critical load to the amount of acid deposition that a particular section of forest is actually receiving. In other words, the deposition index identifies which parts of the state are receiving more acidity than they can handle. Because most of the sulfur and nitrogen in the atmosphere over Vermont arrives on prevailing winds from the south and west, Bennington County receives, in general, more acid deposition than does the Northeast Kingdom.

According to the FMG, the deposition index reveals that 31 percent of the forested landscape in Vermont is now receiving more acidic deposition than the forest can tolerate without declines in nutrients that are essential to plants. Acidification causes nutrients (especially calcium) to be leached out of the soil, which means that more nutrients are being lost than can be replenished by the natural chemical breakdown of minerals in the soil and bedrock. Calcium is a key nutrient in many tree functions and has been shown to be an important part of the process that trees use to avoid freezing injury.

Different tree species have different nutritional requirements. The problems that acid deposition have caused for red spruce, which grows on poor soils at high elevation, are well known. You might think that more-fertile soils—those that host sugar maple, for instance—might be able to tolerate some acidification. They can, but the problem is that sugar maple grows on rich soils for a reason: it needs more calcium than do many of its forest associates, such as beech and birch. This study identified a considerable proportion of Vermont's sugar maple as being at risk. In fact, it may be that sugar maple will be the next tree to show declines at present pollution levels.

Field checks have confirmed that the model's predictions are on the right track. In many cases, areas where deposition

exceeds the critical load do indeed seem to be showing signs of decline and reduced growth. A recent Canadian study confirmed that tree growth is reduced on sites mapped as sensitive but is normal on sites mapped as having a tolerable critical load.

As well as mapping the magnitude of the problem, the FMG's study looks for solutions. If there were a 50 percent reduction in the amount of sulfur and nitrogen that now falls on Vermont forests, 78 percent of the areas currently mapped as sensitive would be mapped as not sensitive. Instead of having 31 percent of the forest destined to decline, only 7 percent would be in that category.

Many experts and forest managers have provided data and reviewed the methods used for this report. Results from much of the rest of the study area (remaining Canadian Provinces, Massachusetts, New Hampshire, Rhode Island, Connecticut, and Maine) were expected to be available in 2004 and 2005. ⌒

Spring Peepers, Winter Sleepers

Michael J. Caduto

In the realm of nature, mysteries often unfold beyond the limits of our perception. Not so with spring peepers. Stand at the edge of any wetland when peepers have reached full voice, and you will be engulfed in the world of another species. A piercing chorus of hundreds of males will wash over your sensory shores. The mating calls of the spring peeper are extraordinarily loud—nature's choir fortissimo.

Peepers awake from their winter slumber, sometimes with snow still on the ground, ready to reproduce. During the previous autumn, the bodies of these tiny chorus frogs began their physiological preparations for the current mating season, a strategy that allows them to start the spring cycle as early as possible. Some males become so well prepared that they begin calling before winter arrives. In my nature journal, I have recorded hearing these "fall peepers" well into foliage season and beyond: one peeper began singing on December 7th, 1998, as the temperature reached the mid-50s.

When autumn wanes and temperatures drop below freezing, how does a one-inch frog survive the winter if all it does is snuggle beneath leaf litter or under a log or tree root? As a peeper's temperature gradually drops, sugars begin to concentrate inside its cells, forming a kind of natural antifreeze. Individual cells expel much of their water so that ice, when it begins to form in small amounts, is confined to the spaces between cells, where its sharp edges won't damage the cell contents of a peeper's internal organs. Still, this strategy only works so well; a dormant peeper will freeze and die at temperatures below about 21°F (−6°C), so insulating snow cover (and a nice blanket of leaves and duff) is crucial.

Even though a spring peeper in winter is dormant and its body is cold, its cells and organs still need some energy to stay alive. But its body is receiving neither the oxygen nor the nutrients that would normally circulate in the blood of an active animal. To get around this, the peeper relies on energy stored the previous autumn. The same sugar that acts as antifreeze in the dormant peeper's cells also serves as a source of nourishment, as do the glycogen reserves stored in its organs. These carbohydrates slowly ferment to provide a bit of energy for the sluggish metabolism of the dormant "peepsicle."

As these carbohydrate supplies dwindle in early spring, peepers wake up and migrate to marshes, bushy swamps, woodland pools, and the edges of ponds. This is the easiest time to find the tiny, light-brown frogs. Look for the dark brown, X-shaped cross that marks their backs and gives rise to the species name of "crucifer." The three-quarter-inch males are smaller than the females, which can grow to be 1¼ inches.

Males start to call as early as mid-March in southern Vermont and New Hampshire. They inflate a dark, olive-colored throat pouch to nearly the size of their body and use it to push air over their vocal cords, repeating this cycle and making a sound both when they inhale and when they exhale. Each piercing call rises in a crescendo. Listen closely to a peeper chorus, and you'll soon realize that the peepers play off each other, engaging in duets, trios, quartets, and more. Sometimes you can hear a birdlike trill, which males use to defend modest mating territories that range from about 4 to 16 inches across.

Peepers have an uncanny knack for positioning themselves so that the surrounding leaves and stems amplify their calls and cause them to seem as if they are emanating from somewhere else—a kind of natural ventriloquism. Combine this with an ability to change the tone of their skin color to match the environment, and it's not surprising that it takes patience and, often, a strong flashlight to actually see a peeper calling.

When a female swims over to a singing male and touches him to indicate her amorous intent, he climbs onto her back and holds on tight as she swims around. Males fertilize up to 800 eggs as the eggs emerge from the female, with the eggs deposited individually or in small clusters on submerged vegetation. Females then retreat from the pond while their diminutive Don Juans continue to serenade for weeks, a few even crooning until the fireflies begin to sparkle.

Peeper populations are healthy throughout New Hampshire and Vermont. They thrive in wetlands and will reproduce as long as the water is not too acidic, requiring a pH above 4. Spring peepers aren't experiencing the widespread growth deformities, such as missing limbs and digits, affecting some other local species of frogs. At the moment, the state of these boisterous and endearing little creatures is as bright as their familiar ringing calls. ∾

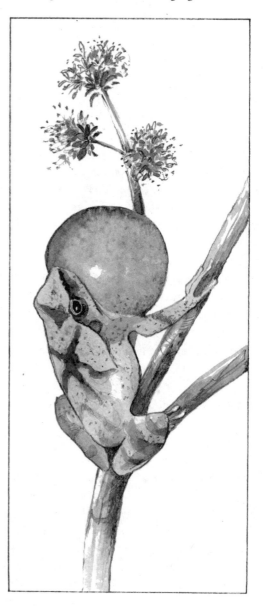

Furlough for a Forbidden Fruit

❧

Virginia Barlow

Chances are you have seen a victim of white pine blister rust. I think it's safe to say that most big dead white pines—the ones with the remains of large crowns, not those that were slowly squeezed out by their neighbors—have this fungus to blame for their demise.

The transportation of tree diseases across the globe is not a new phenomenon. This fungus, one of the first introduced tree diseases (and for white pines, easily the worst), began its journey from its native Russia to North America in 1705. The first move was when our much-admired white pines were shipped from New England to the estate of Lord Weymouth in England. There they were renamed Weymouth pines and, by the mid-1800s, had been widely planted in Europe as well as in England. When a Russian pine infected with blister rust was shipped west, the disease hopped over to European Weymouth pines. The final helping hand was held out to the disease in the late 1800s, when American nurseries ran short of homegrown white pine seedlings to use in reforestation efforts and imported infected Weymouth pine seedlings to several different states.

Blister rust spreads quickly, and by the early 1900s, white pines throughout Vermont and New Hampshire were infected and dying. This fungus is true to its name: it attacks white pine, causes blisters, and has rust-colored spores in one of the stages of its complicated existence.

Five different types of spores are produced during the life cycle of this fungus, and three of them can only survive and reproduce on currants and gooseberries, which make up the genus *Ribes*. The disease does not spread from one pine to another; it must complete part of its life cycle on a *Ribes* plant. Spores produced on the leaves of *Ribes* then travel back to pines and infect the trees by entering the tiny holes in the needles, called stomata.

In an attempt to control the disease, the cultivation of *Ribes* was banned soon after blister rust was introduced, and crews were sent into the woods to tear up wild *Ribes* plants or treat them with herbicides in an attempt to eliminate this link in the chain of infection. If there are no currants or gooseberries close to white pines, there will be no new cases of white pine blister rust. On paper, it looked like a winning strategy.

It is estimated that over $150 million has been spent on destroying *Ribes* to save pines, plus an unknown amount on programs to breed resistance into both white pine and *Ribes*. In 1949, more than $6.5 million was appropriated for *Ribes* eradication. Fifty years ago, 95 percent of the $3.8 million spent on controlling forest diseases was aimed at blister rust.

Eliminating wild *Ribes* in areas where blister rust is most damaging—mainly cold, damp environments—is not effective. If even a few *Ribes* plants survive, the infection rate remains high. Eliminating *Ribes* from nonhazard areas, on the other hand, is unnecessary, because there the disease occurs infrequently, regardless of the number of *Ribes* bushes.

Except in Maine and in the vicinity of tree nurseries, eradication programs have been abandoned as being futile. There are many native *Ribes* species, and their seeds may lie dormant for years before sprouting. To compound the problem, plants can grow back from small pieces of their roots. The federal ban on planting *Ribes* ended in 1966, and many states have cancelled eradication programs. In most states in the Northeast, all laws on the subject have either been rescinded or are not enforced anymore.

However noble the cause, there is bound to be opposition to an expensive program that doesn't always work, especially one that forbids a delicious and nutritious crop from being planted. The pendulum now is swinging to the side that likes currant juice and jelly. Plus, it seems that currant juice is good for you, as well as tasty.

Several *Ribes* varieties have been bred that are resistant to blister rust. The black currants Consort, Coronet, and Crusader do not become infected, and farmers and gardeners throughout the Northeast have expressed an interest in growing them. Some foresters are a little worried about this, pointing out that these resistant cultivars are also non-native species and will inevitably interbreed with native species. The progeny from these crosses will be disseminated across the landscape, and subsequent generations may have little resemblance to their parents with respect to their invasiveness or their resistance to blister rust.

Finding a balance between the goals of forestry and those of farming—with currants being restricted to certain areas, perhaps—will require cooperation and communication. If that happens, we can have both black currant jelly and a nice set of pine shelves on which to store the jars. ❧

Invaders in the Nursery

Anne Margolis

Even though it's cold outside, you may be warmed by the colorful nursery catalogs that seem to arrive in the mail almost daily. But as your eyes drift over the snow-blanketed landscape, envisioning exotic-looking perennials, try to remember just how exotic some of those plants really can be.

Non-native (also called alien or nonindigenous) plants come from elsewhere, but though they are not natural in our ecosystem, they do not necessarily pose a threat to it either. Most will only, at worst, jump the garden border and take hold here and there.

However, a non-native plant can become an invasive plant when it becomes so successful that it outcompetes and displaces our native plants. Invasives cause real havoc in our native ecosystems but nevertheless are often planted as ornamentals and landscape specimens for that very same reason—their vigor.

Invasives are among the most pressing environmental problems today; scientists believe they have contributed to the decline of 42 percent of the species on the federal endangered and threatened species lists. We as gardeners have the responsibility and ability to choose native alternatives, which have evolved along with the other animals and plants that make up our local ecosystem.

For instance, you might be considering a Norway maple for your yard. It is native to Europe and was originally brought here as a landscape plant, but it is so adaptable that it has spread throughout New England on its own. One reason for its success is that (not unlike some native trees) its roots exude a chemical thought to inhibit the growth of any other species under its canopy.

There are many excellent alternatives to the Norway maple, including native red maple (also adaptable to many sites) and yellow birch. Red maple has colorful leaves in the fall and bright red twigs in the winter, and its pinkish buds add the first touches of color to the greening spring landscape. Yellow birch also puts forth early buds, which, along with its seeds and catkins, are a staple for ruffed grouse, red squirrels, and songbirds.

Maybe you're seeking a colorful shrub, like the bright-red, autumn-leaved winged burning bush (not to be confused with eastern burning bush, a shrub with yellow autumn leaves native to the Midwest), or one that produces bright berries, like the Japanese barberry.

Winged burning bush, native to Asia, grows easily and reproduces rapidly but has the potential to become as invasive here as it already is in the mid-Atlantic states, where it crowds out understory plants. Japanese barberry, native to Europe and China, spreads quickly by seeds, which, contained in their fleshy red fruits, are attractive to birds. However, its sharp spines also impede wildlife movement, while the bush itself crowds out many native plants.

Instead of these two intruders, try downy serviceberry, which sports lovely clusters of drooping, fragrant, white flower clusters in spring. Better yet, those flowers become fruits that can be made into excellent jellies, jams, and pies—if you can get to them before the songbirds, turkeys, grouse, doves, foxes, raccoons, and squirrels. Native blueberry and sumac can also fulfill the niche for bright autumn foliage while providing a delicious fall crop.

No discussion of invasive species can ignore purple loosestrife. This beautiful aquatic plant is called "the purple plague" for its ability to reproduce and spread rapidly; it can propagate vegetatively or by the millions of tiny seeds it produces. Once cultivated in gardens, it now chokes wetlands across the country.

Unfortunately, some nurseries are leading people to believe that certain cultivars of loosestrife are sterile. According to Bern Blossey, director of the Biological Control of Non-Indigenous Plants Program at Cornell, "the claim that cultivars of purple loosestrife are sterile is totally false."

Selling, distributing, and transporting purple loosestrife are illegal activities in Vermont and New Hampshire because of the dangers this plant poses. The yellow-flowered garden loosestrife is also considered highly invasive. So instead, consider planting native bee balm, blazing star, common joe-pye weed, figworts, or purple coneflower.

Some other invasives on the most-wanted list are wintercreeper and English ivy (two groundcovers), oriental bittersweet (a fast-growing vine), Chinese and European privet, common and glossy buckthorn, and Japanese, Amur, Morrow's, and Tatarian honeysuckle, which are fast-growing shrubs. Also on the list are Japanese knotweed, coltsfoot, and most common reed (or *Phragmites*) populations, all found in wet areas.

For more information on invasive plants, consult the Invasive Plant Atlas of New England (a database compiled by the University of Connecticut) or contact the New England Wildflower Society, which has put together a great list of native alternatives. Your regional cooperative extension or state agriculture department will also be a great resource. When in doubt, just remember—keep it local! ❧

April

FIRST WEEK

1

Willow pollen is the first spring food
for many species of bees.

Killdeer return. The male and female
look alike and soon both will incubate
the eggs and care for the chicks.

The spirited song of the vesper
sparrow, an early migrant, is often
heard at dusk—hence its name.

Spring peepers reach full volume. Isolated
peepers will peep until November, but only in
the spring is there a big deafening peeper chorus.

Garter snakes may be sunning on
the warmest of warm days.

SECOND WEEK

2

As spring approaches, both male and
female cardinals sing. Usually, just
male songbirds get to do this.

Look for the round holes made by
woodcocks as they probe for earthworms
with their long bills in alder thickets.

Red foxes are giving birth to three to
seven pups. Until the pups open their
eyes, the female leaves the den only
for water, and the male brings food.

The white flowers of bloodroot are out
before the leaves. The origin of its name
will be clear if you scratch the root.

THIRD WEEK

Sapsuckers have returned. Their drumming is distinctive: a series of fast knocks followed by a few slower, erratic ones.

Trout lilies blooming. The pretty yellow flowers follow the sun during the day and close at night.

Poor Sam Peabody, Peabody, Peabody—the plaintive whistle of the white-throated sparrow is heard in brushy and open habitats.

Wild leek leaves are approaching full size. They are delicious to eat now but will yellow and die before the flowers bloom in mid-summer.

FOURTH WEEK

The sweet trill of American toads can be heard at night.

Queen bumblebees fly in a zigzag course close to the ground searching for mouse holes. The queen will begin a new colony in an abandoned mouse nest.

First of perhaps three litters of northern short-tailed shrews is born. This common shrew has a poisonous bite and preys on mice and voles that are larger than it is.

Osprey migration is underway. Look for them along rivers, hovering over open water, or perched on large snags.

Not a Hole in the Ground

Virginia Barlow

Today's vernal pools are a gift of the most recent glacier, the Wisconsin, which retreated 10,000 years ago. The soil beneath them is impermeable, either because it has been compacted by the weight of glacial ice or because it consists of very fine claylike glacial deposits. But vernal pools must have existed prior to the Wisconsin. Because so many species depend on them for their survival, biologists believe that vernal pools have been an important part of the landscape for a very long time.

In late summer or fall, a vernal pool is a big, empty crater, without any trees or shrubs, yet surrounded by a forest of trees. It could look like a wonderfully convenient place to pile brush.

This might have terrible consequences for the many salamanders, frogs, invertebrates, and other animals that mate and reproduce when the pool is filled with water in the spring and early summer—good reason to learn to distinguish a mere hole in the ground from a true vernal pool.

Aside from the absence of trees, the most obvious clue is that the leaves at the bottom of the depression are usually covered with sedi-ment, possibly just a dusty, dry sediment if you were to visit on a dry day.

Vernal pools are best identified by the absence of vegetation, even when they are full of water. While other wetland environments are characterized by the type of vegetation growing in and around them, vernal pools—even in spring, when the ephemeral pool actually is a pool—have no pondweeds, no cattails, and no sedges. On rare occasions, duckweed and other plants that can tolerate drying up will appear.

Just as salmon reproduction is completely dependent on the natal rivers to which the salmon return, the destiny of many amphibians is linked to nearby vernal pools. These small creatures don't usually travel over long distances, so the destruction of just one pool could knock out the whole local population of some species.

Each spring, frogs and salamanders are in a race against time and the sun to develop from eggs to swimming tadpoles to terrestrial adults before these temporary bodies of water dry up. To help vernal pools maintain water throughout the spring, cutting trees nearby is not recommended because this may increase siltation into the pool and reduce its depth. More sunlight and wind will reach the surface, perhaps increasing evaporation and hastening the drying process. Leaving at least a 50-foot uncut buffer on all sides of the pool will preserve shady conditions.

But it is important that vernal pools do dry out at some point over the course of a few years so that creatures such as fish, which depend on the uninterrupted presence of water, don't take up residence and devour all the tadpoles. Dragonfly larvae also love to eat tadpoles and can wrap their powerful mandible around soft-bodied tadpoles that are twice as big as they are. It takes two years for some dragonfly larvae to mature, so dryness at summer's end will wipe out these predators, at least temporarily.

It is possible that ruts in the woods made by skidders or other heavy equipment could also harm salamanders and frogs. If they are lured into laying their eggs in these watery troughs on a rainy April night, and if the inadequate pool dries prematurely, the half-grown tadpoles that are not yet able to venture onto dry land will die.

Steven Faccio, of the Vermont Institute of Natural Science, attached little radio transmitters to adult spotted and Jefferson salamanders as they were leaving vernal pools after they had laid eggs in the spring to see how far they wandered. Most remained within a 500- to 800-foot

radius of their breeding pools, and Faccio believes that ideally all of this habitat should get extra protection. He believes that timber harvesting within this home range may be harmful to salamanders and that as much dead and downed wood as possible should be allowed to accumulate on the forest floor.

Organic matter, especially decaying organic matter, is the bread and butter of the host of organisms on which salamanders feed. Plus, during dry times, larger rotting trunks and branches retain moisture, a feature that is essential to amphibians during all the phases of their lives, not just when they are hanging out at the pool. ∾

Beyond the Pussy Willow

❧

Michael J. Caduto

Soon after moving to Vermont 25 years ago, I began to hear a common lament, delivered with a slow shake of the head and a sigh of Yankee resignation. "There's no springtime here. We go from winter right to summer, not like down south where spring lasts for months."

While our vernal season does move quickly, spring stretches longer here than most people realize. Beyond the first steam that rises from sugaring shacks, the return of red-winged blackbirds, and the calls of wood frogs, there are subtle harbingers awaiting those who seek out our earliest blooms.

Pussy willows, those fuzzy forerunners of full flowers, are a welcome sight in the wetlands of April. A Native American story tells of a rabbit that jumped up into a willow shrub from atop the winter's deepest snows. He was so exhausted from a day of leaping that he nestled in the crotch of a high branch and slept away the rest of the winter. The snows melted. When this Rabbit Van Winkle awoke and looked down from what was then a great height, he became dizzy and fell. As he plummeted, tiny bits of fuzz from his tail caught and tore off on the tips of each branch. Ever since that day, pussy willow flower buds have borne spring coats of fur.

Late snows and freezing rains often cover the outside of each willow bud's jacket, which protects the growing flower parts within. When these flowers mature, they produce a bounty of mustard-colored pollen that is an important food for honeybees, moths, and other insects that buzz from bloom to bloom. These early spring visitors team up with the wind to help spread pollen at a time when there are no leaves to inhibit the breeze that blows through the branches.

If you notice little breaks in the snow cover where pussy willows grow, look for the thick, greenish brown cowling of skunk cabbage, with its purple splotches and veins. Inside the 3- to 6-inch-tall hood is a tight round cluster of flowers. As long as the air temperature is above freezing, this relative of the tropical philodendron and dieffenbachia can maintain a cozy 71.6°F (22°C) within its hood and actually melt its way through the snow. Small flies and honeybees use these heat islands to warm up on foraging flights.

Now grab a pair of binoculars to view another jewel of the plant world: wildflowers on high that sometimes emerge before the pussy willow. Focus up in the branches of silver maple to see its tiny flowers. In Vermont, I have recorded the appearance of the red female blooms and reddish yellow male flowers on the first day of April. A popular shade tree, silver maple grows naturally along the edges of wetlands and rivers. In mid- to late April, when the flowers have gone by, their remnants fall as nondescript squiggly things that pile up on cars and sidewalks. Later in the summer, silver maple seeds detach and spiral down like small whirligigs.

As early as March 31st, American hazelnuts bloom in the filtered shade of hedgerows and in moist forests. The dangling male catkins are easy to find, but you'll need to look backwards through your binoculars—using them as a hand lens—to explore the diminutive female blossoms of this delicate shrub whose petals shoot from the bud like a burst of floral fireworks. It takes three of these crimson beauties, stretched petal-to-petal, to reach across the face of a dime. These flowers will eventually form hazelnuts, or filberts. Young women of colonial America named individual filberts after men they were attracted to and then threw the nuts onto glowing embers. The one that blazed the highest was destined to become her "flame."

Focus again in the treetops to see two of our earliest bloomers. The dangling, fuzzy flowers of popple (also poplar or aspen) precede the familiar quaking, pea-green leaves. I have seen several chunky ruffed grouse roost incongruously in the leafless crowns of aspen and feast on the delicate blooms. Each aspen tree, like holly and willow, bears either male or female flowers. Aspens can also propagate by root sprouts, and sometimes a grove spreads out from one parent tree to form a giant clone. Watch for the cottony tufts that drift down when the mature seeds begin to disperse.

A naturalist I know argues that all of these florid events take a back seat, in both timing and splendor, to the display of our beloved and embattled American elm, whose purplish flowers are among the most precocious. Whichever flower is your favorite, spring begins early and lasts long for anyone who takes the time to develop an eye for the intricate beauty of our first flowers of the season. ∾

Get the Lead Out

Chuck Wooster

What's the first thing you think of when you hear "lead poisoning"? Paint from old houses, perhaps—especially old window frames and sashes? Or maybe, if you're a waterfowl enthusiast, from buckshot or fishing tackle? Both of these are common and well-publicized ways in which lead finds its way into our environment, and both can lead to neurological damage in humans and other animals.

But there's another common source of lead poisoning in humans, one that is particularly likely to affect those of us who live out in the country—out in the clean, rural areas where nobody is thinking about lead poisoning. It's gardening.

Before you panic, here's the good news: lead in the environment is not a widespread, diffuse problem like acid rain or global climate change. Very little "new" lead now finds its way into the environment compared with a generation ago, thanks to various laws like the Clean Air Act. But lead is a relatively big, somewhat inert element that can sit in the soil for decades before it causes a problem. That's why lead in the soil remains a matter of concern for those of us who live and garden in rural areas.

Picture the following tranquil scene: a rustic old farmhouse with lots of flowers growing around it, perhaps an apple tree or two out front, a tidy garden sheltered from the wind by an old foundation wall, and a somewhat dilapidated ell being used as a garage or tractor shed. This is a classic spot—a classic New England farmstead, and classic spot for possible lead poisoning.

Back in the good old days, there were three primary ways for lead to get into the environment, and our tranquil country scene has all three: lead from gasoline, lead from paint, and lead from pesticides. (OK, there was a fourth primary source—lead from smelters—but that's a story for another, more urban, day.)

Tetraethyl lead was added to gasoline between 1924 and 1982 to improve performance and prevent engine knock. Lead carbonate (and related lead compounds) was added to paint from the 1800s up until 1978 to make colors more durable and brilliant. Lead arsenate was a pesticide used as late as 1988 to protect orchards—especially apple trees—from insect damage. It almost goes without saying that the rural parts of New Hampshire and Vermont were no strangers to gasoline, paint, or apple trees.

The good news is that airborne lead, because it is so heavy compared with other common elements and compounds, tends to land on the ground quite close to where it was emitted: within a few dozen feet of the road or driveway, within a few feet of the foundations of houses and barns, and directly underneath apple trees. The bad news is that you can get lead poisoning not only by eating vegetables grown in contaminated soil but also by breathing in lead while working the soil, especially if that soil is heavily contaminated.

The way to avoid lead poisoning from these sources is as simple as not gardening next to the road, the house, or the old orchard. Roads and houses are pretty easy to spot, of course, but figuring out where old orchards or apple trees once stood can be trickier. Any roads, houses, or orchards built or planted in the lead-free days since the mid-1980s shouldn't be a problem anyway.

But what if your prize garden spot happens to be in the foundation of the old barn, or up along the sunny side of your old farmhouse? It's certainly worth the peace of mind to have a simple soil test done to see if you have a problem—visit the website of the Vermont or New Hampshire agricultural extension service for details.

If your site tests positively, all is not lost. If the lead level is just slightly above the dangerous level, grow only flowers, and mulch the soil to keep the lead in the ground and not on you or the flowers. If you have an especially contaminated site, you can remove the top foot or two of soil and replace it with fresh loam from a clean spot somewhere else. Provided your soil hasn't been worked deeply in the past, the lead will still be in the top few inches of soil, right where it landed 20 or 50 or 100 years ago.

But whatever you do, don't give up gardening! The rhubarb is already up, and the first red, juicy, sun-ripened, sun-warmed tomatoes are only 10 weeks away. Just make sure your prize-winning garden vegetables aren't being served up with a side of lead. ◡

Rites of Spring

Ted Levin

hen April temperatures reach 45° Fahrenheit and a long rain extends into the evening, spotted salamanders are awakened by water trickling through the forest soil. They push their way up through the earth and, guided by gravity and a moisture gradient, begin their annual migration down to vernal pools. Vernal pools (literally "spring" pools) are ephemeral. Filled with snowmelt and rain in the spring, they are dry by midsummer. Spotted salamanders depend on vernal pools because they contain no fish, which feed on salamander eggs, tadpoles, and even adults. Once the 6- to 8-inch spotted salamanders reach the water, their dance begins.

The number of salamanders in a single vernal pool can be extraordinary. One year on April 17, in a pool in Norwich (Vermont), a congress of more than 50 male spotted salamanders—their yellow spots gleaming in the beam of my flashlight—twisted and turned on a mat of drowned red maple leaves. When the first female arrived, she approached the group and picked a mate. The two swam away to a less crowded section of the pool and began to circle, cheek to cheek like spinning square-dance partners.

Half an hour later, the male broke away. I followed him with my light to a shallower section of the pool. Here he deposited white conical packets of sperm (spermatophores) on the bottom of the pool. He interrupted this activity twice to rise to the surface for air—legs folded against his sides, propelled by his twisting body and tail.

When the last spermatophore was in place, he swam back to the female and coaxed her into the shallows, leading her directly to the white packets. She straddled the spermatophores and picked them up with the lips of her cloaca, consummating their courtship with prepackaged sex. Retrieving the spermatophores is the closest thing to internal fertilization in the amphibian world. When she was through, the male returned to the congress, and the female, swollen with eggs and carrying sperm, swam off into deeper water, her yellow spots fading in my light beam. Hours later, as six or seven other pairs danced in the shallows, she laid her eggs around a submerged branch.

As the eggs pass out of a female's cloaca, spermatophores rupture, fertilizing the eggs in each tiny mass. In a short time, a gelatinous envelope around each egg cluster absorbs water and swells to the size of a lemon. If air is trapped inside the gel, the egg sac turns milky white. More often it looks green, colored by algae that grow on the outside of the eggs. The algae provide the developing embryos with a rich supply of oxygen and in return thrive on their carbon dioxide wastes.

Jefferson salamanders also migrate to vernal pools but arrive earlier, by a week or more, than the spotted salamanders, while ice still coats the center of the water. Their tadpoles take a longer time to transform than those of the spotteds, and for this reason they prefer cool dark pools, well ahead of the drying sun. There are many Jefferson salamander pools in the higher elevations of northern New England, but these large gray-brown salamanders, sides flecked with blue, are difficult to see, for they seem to vanish in dark water.

Altogether, nine species of salamanders are found in northern New England, and eight are still dependent on water for egg-laying and at least the tadpole stage of their lives. The exception, the lungless redbacked salamander, parted company with its amphibious relatives long ago and now lives its entire life in rich deciduous woodlands. Redbacks lay their eggs in cavities of rotting logs, and the tadpoles grow and metamorphose entirely within the eggs. The young hatch as miniature replicas of their parents.

Northern New England's amphibians can be counted on each spring for a lively nuptial show in which the frogs provide the music and the salamanders the rhythmic and sensuous courtship dance. Frogs, with their well-developed sense of hearing, are brought together at the breeding pools by sound. But salamanders have no middle ear to receive sound and no vocal cords with which to produce it. Instead, their courtship is triggered by ritualized behavior and by odor, as they wag their tails, rub their chins together, and dance together in silence. ∾

The Bird-Coffee Connection

Chris Rimmer

Winter's back has finally broken. Painful memories of subzero temperatures are receding as red-winged blackbird and eastern phoebe songs announce the steady march of spring. Yet, far to our south, the majority of songbirds that grace our woodlands and backyards during spring and summer—thrushes, vireos, warblers, tanagers, and orioles—are just beginning to move northward from their wintering grounds in Latin America.

Sipping our early morning cup of coffee as we contemplate the remnant snowpack outside, most of us eagerly await the arrival of these melodic and brightly plumed songsters. Yet how many of us are aware of the connection between the brew in our cup and the health of migratory bird populations, let alone how our coffee-drinking habits can have a profound impact on their conservation?

Many species of neotropical migrants—birds that spend winters south of the United States—have experienced troubling declines over the past two to three decades. Habitat loss and degradation in Central and South America and the Caribbean have put the squeeze on populations of many long-distance migratory birds. Some of our most common and beloved summer residents—such as the wood thrush and rose-breasted grosbeak—are in trouble. Scientists and conservationists are worried.

Want to help in a small but significant way? Drink coffee! Just pay careful attention to the type of coffee you drink.

Coffee is by nature a shade-loving shrub that evolved in the tropical forests of modern-day Ethiopia. Now the second most traded commodity in the world (after oil), it is the single most important crop for many Latin American and Caribbean countries. For centuries, coffee was grown in these countries under the shaded canopies of native trees, thus simulating a natural forest and supporting a rich diversity of flora and fauna, including migratory birds. Scientists have identified up to 150 species of migrants—including familiar Vermont and New Hampshire breeders like ruby-throated hummingbirds, black-throated green warblers, American redstarts, and indigo buntings—using shaded coffee plantations in Guatemala and Mexico. These numbers are similar to those found in undisturbed forests.

Many tropical resident birds, such as tinamous, parrots, trogons, toucans, and woodcreepers, also thrive in shade coffee plantations. But birds are only one indicator of shade coffee's role in protecting biological diversity. Studies of insects, canopy trees, orchids, and amphibians show that shade coffee plantations often serve as critical refuges for forest-dependent species in areas where natural forests have been lost or greatly diminished.

The traditional practice of growing shaded coffee has given way in recent decades to a system of "full-sun" farming, which produces higher yields. Most coffee plantations in Brazil, Colombia, and Costa Rica have now been cleared of overstory shade trees. The sun-tolerant coffee varieties come at great ecological cost, causing increased soil erosion and requiring constant doses of chemical fertilizers, pesticides, herbicides, and fungicides. They are not sustainable without intensive management, and individual plants must be replaced much more frequently than the shade varieties.

In addition to these agronomic risks, full-sun coffee production has resulted in major habitat changes for migratory birds. Plantations are biological deserts compared to their traditional shade counterparts; studies have shown that there are 94–97 percent fewer bird species in sun-coffee farms than on shaded farms.

Many coffee farmers in the neotropics would prefer to maintain shade trees on their plantations as their parents and grandparents did, but they are under great political and economic pressure to convert to full-sun farms. Government agencies often subsidize the transition, and coffee prices are largely controlled by fluctuations in production in Brazil and Colombia, leaving farmers at the mercy of international market forces.

As concerned coffee drinkers, nature enthusiasts, and conservationists, we can each make a difference. We need to be aware of the impact of coffee production on tropical forests and wildlife, and we should support Latin American and Caribbean coffee growers who maintain shade trees on their farms, thereby protecting the wintering habitat of North American migrant birds. The Rainforest Alliance, along with a number of other conservation organizations, has developed a process to identify and certify shade-grown coffee that is grown in an environmentally sustainable manner.

As consumers, we can request that local suppliers carry or serve certified shade-grown coffee as an alternative to commercial brands, nearly all of which are grown in full sun. Ask for it! The benefits to the migrant birds that are now winging their way back to northern New England—as well as to a host of other wildlife, tropical forest flora, and local people themselves—will be great. As you sit on your deck in a few weeks sipping coffee while the wood thrushes and scarlet tanagers sing, make sure your brew is shade grown! ∽

The Fleeting Trout Lily

Virginia Barlow

By early June, when the growing season seems to be just getting up to speed, some of our most beautiful woodland wildflowers will have already come and gone. To find any sign of trout lily, spring beauty, squirrel corn, Dutchman's breeches, dwarf ginseng, or toothwort in July, you will have to do some digging, for by then their leaves will have shriveled up and disappeared.

Though these plants are often called "spring ephemerals," which suggests that they are short-lived, all of these are hardy perennials with underground storage organs that live throughout the year. They exploit a niche, like everyone else, but for these plants the niche is a temporal one: between snowmelt and the time when deciduous trees leaf out. During this period, the forest floor is moist, nutrient-rich, and so sun-drenched that it warms quickly.

Although the length of this spring niche varies from year to year, depending mostly on the amount of snow, it is always very brief. The ephemerals' growth is limited by low temperatures at the beginning and by increasing shade in late May. When hardwood leaves come out, it is like pulling a window shade on the forest floor.

At that point, spring ephemerals close up shop, but, like a successful toy shop at Christmas, they will have amassed enough working capital to make it to the next season. They shut down before losing money, and they stash their savings underground. Also, like the toy shop, preparation for the hectic season begins well before the new infusion of income is at hand. They spend the winter preparing and by spring are ready to make the most out of the sun and warmth of early spring days.

All the ephemerals have conspicuous, insect-pollinated flowers, but you don't have to be a honeybee to appreciate them. They all are beautiful and bloom at a time of year when there is not a lot of floral competition.

Trout lily is the most common spring ephemeral. The pale yellow flowers with five curled-back petals are small for lilies, only about one inch across. The leaves are sort of trout shaped, as well as having a mottled, troutlike pattern of brown splotches.

Only about one-half of one percent of the individual plants in a bed of trout lilies will flower in a given year. Normally, it takes many years for a plant to accumulate enough resources to be able to produce a flower, and most never do, persisting in a subflowering state for years before dying.

Trout lilies have been dug up, weighed, measured, and analyzed at all times of the year, and some of the statistics gleaned from these depredations are eyebrow raising. In one study, the average dry weight of the plants increased by over 250 percent in just 12 days. Over the whole growing season, which was 37 days in the year of the study, the dry weight increased by nearly 450 percent.

Even so, trout lilies won't win any prizes for being the world's fastest-growing plants. They do, however, photosynthesize and grow considerably faster than forest-floor plants that stay green throughout the summer. Weight losses during the long nonphotosynthetic period can equal or exceed the dramatic gains of spring.

Although trout lilies make up only a very small fraction of the biomass of the forest, their capacity for extremely rapid growth over a short period plays a significant role in preserving the nutrient capital of the forest ecosystem. The greatest soil nutrient losses occur in spring because, until the trees leaf out, their roots do not absorb nutrients. In spring, seepage from the nutrient-rich soil is more likely to be carried away from the forest ecosystem and into streams than at any other time of year.

But it's trout lilies to the rescue, for this is when they are growing most actively. They temporarily accumulate nutrients, especially potassium and nitrogen, when these elements are in abundance and when other growing plants are in short supply. Trout lily leaves contain more nitrogen than summer green plants,

an indication that they take advantage of the higher soil-nitrogen levels in spring.

About seven weeks after trout lily leaves have unfurled, the green parts begin to die. Some of the nutrients are transferred from the leaf to the corm. The rest are released as the leaf decomposes. But by this time, the roots of trees and other plants are actively growing and can make good use of them.

It is satisfying to think that these beautiful little plants, plants that you might think could get by just on their good looks, are also making a contribution to the trees that tower over them. Look for them this month on your favorite hardwood hillside. ∾

May

❧

FIRST WEEK

Hills are turning startling new colors: light pea
green, and pinkish and reddish greens, as almost
all the trees except ash unfurl their buds.

Juncos are building nests of dried grass.
They will line them with deer hair.

Fairy shrimp are carrying eggs
in woodland pools.

Marsh marigolds are blooming.

Spring azure butterflies, which are silvery
violet-blue above, flit through the woods,
signaling the return of warm weather.

SECOND WEEK

Wood thrush nests are being built in three layers,
usually about 10 feet off the ground. Leaves,
mosses, grasses on the outside, mud in the
middle, and fine rootlets for a lining.

The pointy, coiled spathes of Jack-
in-the-pulpit are opening.

Don't get discouraged about your
lawn: dandelion flowers can be
dipped in flour, fried, and eaten.

New shoots of Japanese knotweed are edible
when less than 8 inches high, perhaps the
best use for this invasive, non-native plant.

THIRD WEEK

3

Starflower, a low plant found in the north
around the globe, is blooming.

Returning hummingbirds will sometimes hover
repeatedly exactly where last year's nectar feeder
was positioned, even if you haven't put it up yet.

Many defoliating insects' eggs are timed
to hatch when tree leaves unfurl, a fact
well known to the many warblers now
arriving to pick off the tender larvae.

Arrival of black flies, for the 180 millionth time.
They've been around since the mid-Jurassic.

FOURTH WEEK

4

Lilacs are in full bloom, and so are grapes, Virginia
creeper, highbush cranberry, pin cherry, hawthorn,
nannyberry, and red osier dogwood.

A male leopard frog's call sounds like a long
snore, lasting up to three seconds, but these
frogs make several other sounds as well.

Most newborn fawns are walking and
nursing when less than one hour old.

The olive-sided flycatcher has a loud and
penetrating call, sometimes described as
a melodious whistle of *whip-three-beers*.

Holey Alliance

Joan Waltermire

The first dawn volley of a yellow-bellied sapsucker on our metal roof is exciting because it signals spring. The twenty-first volley is a little harder to be enthusiastic about, but I forgive them and begin to think "hummingbird."

Ruby-throated hummingbirds arrive at my house in Vershire, Vermont, by early May, which in the past has always made me vaguely uneasy. At that time of year, what was fueling their flashing aerial combats? Columbine nectar? It seemed impossible, and it was. The answer turned out to be sap from sapsucker holes. In fact, in the north, hummingbirds are found only where these oddball woodpeckers live.

In spite of its name, the sapsucker's yellow belly is not very noticeable. A better field mark is its red throat and cap, as it is the only member of the woodpecker family to wear red in both places. Sapsuckers breed and spend their summers all across the northern United States and winter as far south as Mexico and the Caribbean.

But even if you don't know a yellow-bellied sapsucker from a hole in a tree, you probably know its work. Males and females both drill horizontal bands of small holes into the suc-culent inner bark of trees and then feed on the nutrient-rich sap that collects in the holes, as well as on insects attracted to the sap. It is these sapsucker "wells" that feed our hummingbirds in early spring before there are flowers. Although I haven't seen figures on spring sap, one study found that summer sap had a sugar concentration of 16 percent by weight, which is high enough to support hummingbirds without any other sources of nutrients.

In one of those happy confluences of observation and book-learning, I saw this hummingbird-sapsucker relationship in action one fine summer day. An immature sapsucker was flying clumsily from tree to tree in our yard, taking desultory whacks at tree limbs. There was something endearing and comical about her ineptness that kept my interest. Suddenly I noticed that a hummer was flying in attendance. He perched on nearby branches and followed her closely in four flights before giving up.

Sapsucker wells feed other species also. Sap-drinkers in our area include the hairy woodpecker (downies drill their own sap wells), both species of nuthatches, ruby-crowned kinglet, northern waterthrush, pine siskin, goldfinch, white-crowned sparrow, cardinal, and flying, red, and gray squirrels, plus a number of warblers, including the yellow-rumped, black-throated blue, black-throated green, pine, and Cape May. Nondrinking freeloaders such as the crested and least flycatchers, eastern phoebe, robin, and warbling vireo feed on swarms of insects attracted to the sap. Sapsuckers are insect-eaters themselves, especially when feeding fast-growing young, and they devour the larch sawfly, among other pests.

Insect visitors at sapsucker wells in early spring include white-faced hornet queens, who have overwintered and are just emerging from hibernation. Like birds, the queens get energy by drinking the sap and also come to the wells to catch protein-rich insect prey to feed their young. One observer often finds hornet nests below sapsucker licks, perhaps a mutually beneficial arrangement. Such hornets need to keep a sharp eye out for falling objects from above; a sapsucker sometimes gets tipsy from drinking fermented sap and falls from its tree!

In spring, sapsuckers tap the sap of hemlock, aspen, maple, and elm—all early flowerers. Their summer staples are birches, and they can cause significant damage to economically valuable yellow birch. According to one authority on northeastern woodpeckers, sapsuckers drill most heavily on trees that are already wounded. He found the greatest activity on trees with obvious trunk wounds or fungal conks. However, they also drill, although more lightly, on apparently healthy trees, and it seems probable that this helps maintain a subsequent supply of wounded feeder trees.

This hole-drilling is regretted by people who make their living from harvesting trees, but no one proposes to control it. The sapsucker's impact on forest health in New England is a complicated story because its feeding

and nest excavation benefit so many other species. Chickadees, great crested flycatchers, and nuthatches, for example, sometimes nest in old sapsucker nest holes because they lack the beak equipment to make good nest holes of their own. Flying squirrels, deer mice, and red squirrels also find them handy housing. And these are just a few examples. In fact, the sapsucker's influence is so widespread that its loss could cause a cascade of changes in the ecosystem.

But back to the metal roof. Why exactly do sapsuckers whack away at roofs, stovepipes, antennas, and metal gates at this time of year? To attract mates, establish territories, and, it would seem, make sure that nearby humans don't oversleep and miss all the action. ∽

Hummingbird illustration courtesy of the author.

The Misunderstood Garter Snake

Alan Pistorius

"I see a garter snake in my yard once in a while," an editor once complained to me, "but it's never *doing* anything." It's true that snakes live about as privately as sizable above-ground, day-active animals can live, and most people pass a lifetime—many contentedly—without witnessing any of the really interesting stuff.

Sex, for example. Lovemaking for most snake species is a calm and dignified affair, but garter snakes have a better way. Males leave the communal winter dens—anything from rodent burrows and anthills to rock fissures and old farm wells—in early spring and simply hang out. Females emerge later, a few at a time, and immediately become the object of multiple attentions. The resulting "mating ball," a writhing mass of 10 or 20 or more intertwined and feverishly preoccupied snakes, creeps blindly forward like a slow-motion rugby scrum.

It's a miracle that pregnancy ever occurs, given that the unique snake anatomy makes sex almost impossible. And it isn't just the lack of limbs. Male snakes are saddled with a primitive double copulatory organ—the hemipenes—which, under normal circumstances, lies inside the vent through which it must protrude for mating, and pointed the wrong way!

The garter snake solves this anatomical fix with breathtaking ingenuity. Through a combination of propulsor and retractor muscles attached to each hemipenis, one or the other achieves protrusion via eversion: the organ literally turns itself inside out in order to leave the body and connect with a female.

Like some mammals during rut, garter snakes do little or no feeding during the extended spring revelries, nor do they when they gather again near the winter dens in fall. Summer, on the other hand, is all about eating, and garters—unlike sit-and-wait opportunists such as rattlesnakes—are active foragers. I have shadowed garters on these hunting forays. An animal's strategy is simply to meander about the landscape at half-speed—the head raised and swinging from side to side, steely eyes alert, tongue flicking—the animal insinuating itself through (and over, and under) grass clump and duff and blowdown and rock pile in that uncanny serpentine silence. Garters use both conventional smell and the chemoreceptor-rich roof-of-the-mouth Jacobson's organ to trail prey, but mostly they score by simply bumping into a victim. And they nearly have to bump into it: a snake hears little of use on the hunt, nor is its eyesight acute.

It may well fail to notice a motionless frog a foot away.

While some of North America's 13 species of garter snakes hunt in a particular habitat for particular prey, the common garter, among others, is a generalist. It explores streams, marshes, woods damp and dry, mountain slopes, fields and meadows, parks and residential areas, where, in addition to the staples (usually worms and amphibians), it feeds opportunistically on fish, leeches, small birds and rodents, and insects. Garters don't always get much to eat, but since they slow their metabolic rate when inactive, they don't require much. Indeed, physiologists have determined that, during the active season, a Vermont snake needs only about one-twentieth as much food as a same-weight mammalian predator.

Most people think of the *Thamnophis* as small snakes, and several species are. But most of our garters are medium-sized snakes, and females of our common garter may exceed four feet in length. Unlike birds and mammals, reptiles grow—though slowly after reaching sexual maturity—all their lives, and the reason most of us never encounter a large garter snake is that few live long enough to attain much size. A population ecology study in Kansas determined survivorship rates for the common garter at 36 percent for the first year and a constant 50 percent after adulthood is attained at two years. Of 100 newborns, then, something like 18 survive two years and only a single individual lives to age six. So much for large—read teenaged—garter snakes.

What happens to the unfortunate 99 during those six years? Coyote, fox, opossum, the weasel tribe, and domestic animals (dogs, hogs) all kill snakes, as do crows, herons, and hawks. (American kestrels feed large numbers of garters to their young.) Snakes feed on snakes as well, as do turtles and fish. The northern winter poses additional problems. Some young snakes fail to locate safe hibernacula, and dehydration—more so than cold—is a constant threat in the best dry winter dens.

Then, of course, there are humans, whether in the guise of a shopping-mall developer or ophiophobic suburbanite or country dweller with a spade. Or inattentive (even malevolent) motorist. Reptiles and amphibians have never been much good at figuring out roads, and while frogs and salamanders take their big hit while moving to the breeding pools during spring rains, snakes take theirs during the lazy days of October, when too many innocently bask on sun-warmed roads near winter dens. ᴖ

In Praise of Blackflies

∾

Bill Amos

Hoping to avoid what is intolerable, we seek shelter, wrap head, wrists, and ankles, apply evil-smelling concoctions, and sometimes employ a vocabulary best left unused in company. It is blackfly season, a time of attacks behind our ears, under watchbands, and down our socks. Picnics and dispositions are ruined.

But it's only the adults that plague us, and then only the females.

An efficient bloodsucker, the awful adult female blackfly uses chemically sophisticated saliva to keep blood from clotting while she drinks her fill. It is this saliva that arouses our body chemistry to inflammation. Her sense of survival causes her to bite precisely where we are least likely to notice her presence. Then, with inflated body, she flies off to rest and digest the meal, an elusive little Dracula. The males? Inoffensively mild little creatures who sip nectar from flowers.

And at the larval stage, the blackfly deserves our admiration. Anyone examining a brook has seen them, not realizing their identity. Find a riffle where water flows over a flat rock before plunging into a pool. In swift water on the brink of that rock, dozens of dark, twig-like objects bend downstream from the force of the current, each a quarter of an inch long. They could be anything—plants perhaps. Look more closely.

Here is an elongated, brownish insect larva, club-shaped, with bulbous end attached to the rock. At the narrow upper end, two fringed appendages protrude from a small dark head. A circlet of hooks on the swollen bottom of the larva grip a mat of silk attached to the rock's surface. This is the insect's home plate.

The seed-shaped head has chewing jaws with scale-like teeth, a scattering of four simple eyespots, a pair of antennae, and those two specialized limbs. The tip of each of these appendages is equipped with a fan of about 50 curved bristles that unfolds in the flowing water. When an edible morsel is snared by the bristles, it is thrust into the mouth and swallowed. A brook may appear crystal clear, but it transports enough organic matter to feed a multitude of inhabitants. Blackfly larvae have little to do but wait for a meal to arrive.

Harboring a grudge against blackflies, you dislodge a larva and watch it whirl away downstream to what you hope is oblivion. Be prepared for a surprise. A foot or two away, the little insect suddenly defies the laws of physics and stops dead in the racing water. Astonishingly, it begins to move slowly back upstream until it reaches its silken mat. Secure again, it extends head fans and begins feeding as though nothing unusual has happened. What miracle is this? When dislodged, it spins a silken lifeline, one end of which remains attached to the mat. From huge, body-long salivary glands, it pays out silk until safely out of harm's way, then stops, grasps the thread in its jaws, and begins "reeling in" by eating the strand of silk. No wonder adult blackfly populations are so large: there aren't many predators in a brook capable of catching their larvae.

The life stages of a blackfly resemble those of many insects. A female enters the water to lay 500 or so eggs, sometimes choosing instead a wet leaf along the stream bank. With a pointed "egg burster" on its head, each tiny larva soon hatches and creeps to find a place of attachment in the swift water. It feeds, molts up to nine times, and then, before transforming into a flying insect, enters a nonfeeding stage, a blackish, hump-shaped little pupa inside a streamlined silken cocoon. Two sets of feathery gills trail downstream to extract oxygen from the water while metamorphosis takes place.

Transformation complete, the pupal case splits at the head and the new adult, encased in a bubble of air emitted from under its skin, whirls off downstream, instantly rising to the surface. The bubble bursts, and, with hairy, water-repellent feet, the tiny insect runs across the water to a plant or shoreline where it dries its wings and flies away—homing in on that vulnerable spot behind your ear (remember, only females do this). In its genes, a message developed over millennia of being swatted says that thin-skinned hairlines are safe places to find a meal.

Why not sing the praise of this scourge of the North Country, this remarkable creature with an obscure origin in upland brooks? Swat adults if you must. But if for no reason other than its extraordinary specialty for survival in a turbulent watery world, the larval blackfly is worthy of our wonder. ⌒

Roads Affect Female Turtles More

ᕲ

Kent McFarland

The turtle was lying on the white line marking the road edge as I pulled my car over to move it. It was a small painted turtle, and its shell had a deep crack across it. She was taking her last breaths.

I suspected that this was a female before I even got a good look at her, but a close look at her tail confirmed my suspicion. Most turtles wandering away from water at this time of year are females searching for a good place to lay eggs. Many cross roadways and never make it to a nesting site.

I wondered if these accidents were having a detrimental effect on turtle populations, so I contacted Dr. James Gibbs from State University of New York College of Environmental Science and Forestry, who has been studying the problem of adult turtle mortality and its effects on turtle populations overall.

"Most turtle species cannot tolerate much adult mortality, but we had no idea how many turtles were crossing roads and whether road mortality represented a serious threat or not," said Gibbs. "So we modeled turtle movements in a computer as a first attempt to frame the problem, and it indicated that road mortality could indeed be a problem." The model, published in the journal *Conservation Biology*, predicted that road networks typical of the Northeast have the potential to limit turtle populations.

"A breeding adult female turtle is a very valuable component of a local population," noted Dr. Greg Shriver, a former student of Gibbs' who now works at the Marsh-Billings-Rockefeller National Historical Park in Woodstock, Vermont. Adult turtles live long lives and have delayed sexual maturity. Contrast turtles with rabbits, for example, to get an idea of a species that reproduces early and often and for whom, therefore, the survival of each individual adult female is less crucial.

Road networks, meanwhile, are becoming busier and larger. Recently, the Vermont Fish and Wildlife Department's (VFWD) Nongame and Natural Heritage Program newsletter, *Harmonies*, reported that during the past 10 years, Vermont's human population has grown 8.2 percent while at the same time the number of registered vehicles has increased 24 percent. Vermont has over 14,000 miles of roads, and the Vermont Agency of Transportation (VTrans) estimates that the number of vehicle miles traveled by Vermonters is growing seven times faster than the population.

Has that kind of growth in Vermont, let alone other regions of the Northeast, affected turtle populations over the years? "Unfortunately, yes," says Gibbs. "The real issue is that roads are getting more impenetrable every year to animals trying to cross them." The more cars there are on the roads, the more likely a collision becomes.

In a separate study, Gibbs and his student David Steen found that the proportion of males in turtle populations has increased linearly with the expansion of road networks and traffic use. States and regions with higher road densities and more people have fewer female turtles.

Gibbs and Steen teamed up to gather field evidence by examining painted turtle and snapping turtle populations in wetlands with low road densities and others with high road densities. As predicted, both species had male-biased sex ratios in wetlands adjacent to high road densities. Females like the one I found are likely being killed on roadways during annual nesting migrations—a harrowing journey that male turtles do not make.

While this problem may not be as severe in the rural corners of Vermont and New Hampshire as it is in more densely populated areas, it could still threaten some populations. "Even though this region has a lower road density on the landscape than other places, the traffic volume is high enough to still cause mortality that could result in turtle population declines. I am always surprised to see road kill on dirt roads while mountain biking in Vermont, indicating that it does not take too

many vehicles passing by to cause mortality," notes Shriver.

In an effort to address these fatal encounters, an interagency wildlife-crossing team was recently established by VTrans, consisting of trained VTrans employees and several VFWD biologists, to identify areas of high mortality. The team is creating a statewide map and database for wildlife crossings, habitat, road mortality, and transportation information. It will be used to identify significant wildlife corridors associated with state and town roads and assist in future planning.

"When roads are reengineered, crossing barriers or tunnels, as appropriate, can be installed. This is where mitigation is headed, and it's in a very positive direction," said Gibbs.

"Avoiding road crossings, or actually stopping turtles from moving across the road, can really make a difference," said Shriver. It was too late for the turtle I found, but the future might be a little brighter for others. ∽

Nature's Other Silk: Spider Webs

Bill Amos

Even if we shun the leggy creatures that make them, we marvel at the geometric precision and dew-frosted beauty of spider webs. There is nothing so elegant, so versatile, and so perfectly suited to its function as a spider's web. In early mornings at this time of year, there is a glint of webbing on the lawn, and hillsides are decorated with gossamer. There is magic in the scene.

How do spiders create these masterpieces? A spider produces silk from several different kinds of glands, with each gland responsible for its own protein chemistry. These glands are never depleted, because even when web-building is at fever pitch, new proteins are constantly being made. Some spiders can produce up to 2,000 feet of continuous thread, and a mere thousand feet is no big deal for many others.

While still in the gland, the secretion that becomes silk is a thick, water-soluble fluid, but when drawn through spinnerets on the spider's abdomen, its molecular arrangement changes into a tightly packed formation that is insoluble and 10 times denser than the fluid state. The faster a thread is drawn out, the tighter its molecules cling together and the stronger the strand. Despite being a very fine filament, spider silk is so enormously strong that scientists have calculated a strand would have to be 50 miles long before it would break under its own weight. A thread of spider silk has greater tensile strength than steel of the same diameter, at the same time being so elastic that it can stretch more than 25 percent its normal length before breaking.

Some threads are sticky, others are not. They can be fine and delicate or strong and thick. Each type is important to a spider's needs. Spider silk never dries out, doesn't decay from bacterial action, and won't become moldy. Under sheltered conditions, a web may last far longer than the spider itself.

It's tempting to assume that spinnerets are simple nozzles, which they may have been in ancestral spiders, but today they possess complicated valves and muscles and much interior plumbing. Certain species have long spinnerets that almost seem like appendages.

If you study a spider while it spins a web, you'll find the animal doesn't reposition its body in order for silk to come out at an angle. Its spinnerets busily point this way and that, sometimes coordinated, sometimes working independently, all with a common purpose.

Silk is not ejected under pressure, but instead must be drawn out by external means:

wind, gravity, or the spider's movement. A dragline, for example, is first attached to a surface, then the spider walks away or drops into the air to dangle on a lifeline. It may lower itself further, regulating speed and distance, and can plummet all the way to the ground if disturbed. It may scramble back to its former perch, gathering and consuming protein-rich silk as it goes. After eating its webbing, a spider recycles this valuable material; digestion is so quick that the molecular protein building blocks are ready for new silk production in only half an hour.

The familiar orb web is the most sophisticated of all designs: a marvel of construction, but simple in concept. It is a diaphragm, a drumhead, secured around its perimeter, but free to vibrate in the center—which is where the spider usually resides. When an insect hits an outer portion of the diaphanous disk, vibrations travel to the center. The spider instantly knows in which direction to head and dashes out along the nonsticky radial threads. The victim is firmly held by globs of stickiness on the circumferential threads until the spider arrives.

Some species of orb builders don't stay on the web itself but instead attach a "telegraph" line to the sheet of webbing and then sit in a nearby bush, holding the line taut. The web diaphragm vibrates, the message is transmitted, and the spider descends and speeds out on the correct radius to secure its dinner.

The simplest sort of webbing is perhaps the most important. Ballooning allows many kinds of spiders to disperse around the world, wafted on air currents across the widest oceans and highest mountains. When conditions are right, young spiders ascend any available elevation, spin a few short strands of silk, feel the tug of the wind, and let go. I once watched airborne spiders descend on a mid-Pacific island from a continent 2,000 miles away, and I remember an astonishing day right here in Vermont when the cloudless sky sparkled with pinpricks of light. It was a sight so eerie and mysterious, my skin shivered in goose bumps—until it prickled with hundreds of tiny spiderlings alighting on me to seek their way in the world. ∾

Twilight of the Elms

Ginny Barlow

"If you want to be recalled for something that you do, you will be well advised to do it under an Elm—a great Elm, for such a tree outlives the generations of men; the burning issues of today are the ashes of tomorrow, but a noble Elm is a verity that does not change with time."

Even as Donald Culross Peattie—the most eloquent admirer trees have ever had—was writing this in the late 1940s, the elm was changing, and changing for the worse. Dutch elm disease had been introduced to this country in 1930 when a shipment of European elm burlwood arrived at a veneer mill in Ohio. Peattie recognized the disease as a serious threat, but he could not have imagined how truly catastrophic it would become. And bad as the situation was in his day, it got even worse when a more virulent strain of the disease appeared in the 1960s.

Indeed, many memorable things have been done under elms. George Washington is said to have taken command of the Continental Army in July 1775 under an elm in Cambridge, Massachusetts, and Peattie, a better friend to trees than to people, is delighted to discover that the famous tree was but a sapling at the time. "Washington," he says, "is perhaps the only man who ever added stature to an Elm."

Though American cities have unkindly been described as places "where they cut down all the trees and then named the streets after them," elms benefited from urbanization more than any other tree species. Elms have been planted in every kind of habitation, from tiny villages to the largest city. Elm-lined streets practically defined nineteenth-century America.

Some magnificent specimens do survive here and there across Vermont and New Hampshire, often on town greens or in front of old houses, and their grandeur is undeniable. But after a moment of awe beneath the towering fountain of foliage an American elm produces, there is always a question: How long can it last?

Best to go back in time, back to when elms had just the usual afflictions, like other trees. To the time when early settlers chose house sites near elms, knowing that the soil there would be moist and fertile. Then they razed all the other trees, keeping just an elm or two. The shade of elm, from high above the roof, is perfect. Its leaves decompose rapidly and are nutrient rich, and the tree is considered to be a "soil improving" species.

Though the wood has its well-known faults (try splitting it, for instance), it was made into a great assortment of objects in earlier days. Liquids seep out of barrels made from elm, but the wood is perfect for the slack barrels that were filled with flour, butter, sugar, and cheese. Elm wood is easily steam-bent and was used for the hoops for all kinds of barrels. The wood is almost white and imparts no taste, so it was preferred for a variety of domestic utensils, boxes, baskets, crates, iceboxes, washboards, and for the white, scrubbed kitchen table found in almost every farm kitchen. For a time, elm was the most sought-after tree on the market.

Now, thanks to Dutch elm disease, elms rarely reach a merchantable size, but neither is the market for barrels and washboards what it used to be. Small elms are still common along roadsides because the two beetle species that carry the disease from tree to tree don't find young elm bark suitable for egg-laying. They only move in when the bark begins to form fissures.

The skeletons of long-dead elms can still be found along the edges of old fields and pastures, though with the disease having been with us for nearly three-quarters of a century, even these are now rotting away.

If you do come across an American elm, the leaves are oval and lopsided, with small teeth superimposed on larger teeth at the margins, and the veins seldom fork. The twigs are often decidedly zigzagged. If you break off a bit of bark, you will see alternating light and dark layers, remembered by many students as being like a ham-and-cheese sandwich.

Elm flowers appear early in spring, well before the leaves, and give a lovely, light purplish color to the tree. The small, oval, winged fruits fall in late spring and usually germinate within a week or two. Millions of elm seeds do fall and do grow, and between these and the intense efforts of growers and researchers, it is possible to hope that Dutch elm disease can be circumvented somehow and that beautiful 100-foot, vaselike trees will someday arch again across the roads and yards of New England. Perhaps elms will even add stature to the deeds of man once again. ᔕ

June

FIRST WEEK

Hatching time for Hexagenia, our largest
mayfly and a trout favorite.

Hermit thrushes, catbirds, and yellowthroats
continue to sing well after dusk.

Beginning of firefly displays. Also
called lightning bugs, these insects
are really beetles, not flies or bugs.

Honeybee lore: A swarm in June
is worth a silver spoon.

Star-nosed moles are giving birth to three to seven
young. These wetland creatures will soon be eating
worms, insects, leeches, crustaceans, and mollusks.

SECOND WEEK

Black locust flowers produce copious
nectar and are abuzz with bees.

Poison ivy flowers are producing abundant
nectar. It makes good honey.

Female snapping turtles leave the relative
safety of ponds to find a nest site. They
are highly vulnerable on land, which may
account for their reputation as meanies.

Though the woodchuck can be a major nuisance
in the garden, keep in mind that other animals such
as cottontails, weasels, and red foxes use its burrows.

THIRD WEEK

3

Throughout the summer, oyster mushrooms
grow in large, overlapping clusters following
wet weather. Oftentimes shiny, black beetles
get to these choice fungi before you do.

Bobolinks are nesting in meadows and
pastures. Listen for the effervescent song
of the male as he flies up from the grass.

Male smallmouth bass are guarding their nests
in the sandy shallows of lakes and ponds.

Little brown bats are giving birth. Usually
they have one offspring, occasionally two.

FOURTH WEEK

4

Common daylilies are flowering; a mark
that spring has changed to summer.

Now that summer fruits like strawberries
and raspberries are ripening, bears
will begin to gain weight.

Luna moths are drawn to lights, and if
the porch light is on, one may be found
sleeping on the screen door the next day.

Thistle seeds are the goldfinch's favorite
food, and the birds line their nests with the
seeds' down; plus, the colors of goldfinches
and purple thistles go together well.

Ants on Plants

Norah Lake

By June, even in a year with a late spring, the wine-colored spikes of peony flowers have pushed their way back into the aboveground world. These spikes will soon be covered with swelling green knobs of buds. And covered with ants.

It can be a shock for gardeners to find dozens of ants crawling around on one of our most beloved spring garden flowers. Far from causing trouble or harming the flowers, however, these ants are an essential part of the peony's flowering: no ants, no flowers.

The ants are drawn to the tightly furled peony flowers by a sweet nectar exuded from the waxy, red-rimmed bud scales. In return for this high-energy food, the nectar-seeking ants gently probe the clenched petals, loosening the folds and helping the flowers open. Some gardeners say the ants only encourage and hasten a process that would otherwise happen on its own, while others insist that, without the ants eating away the waxy scales and traipsing between the petals, the buds would not be able to open at all.

In either case, the ants also guard the peonies against harmful insect pests that would otherwise damage the plants and diminish the ants' proprietary nectar supplies, leaving gardeners with nothing more than chewed, unopened buds. The moral of the story: set aside the pesticide; far from being a problem, these ants are part of the solution.

Ants and peonies together form a mutualism, a type of symbiotic relationship that is beneficial and often essential to both of the parties involved. Mutualisms have evolved between many plants and animals over thousands of years of living together in the same habitat, leading to species with specialized and co-dependent interactions. With these mutualisms driving the inner workings of many natural systems, even the most insubstantial-seeming species such as ants—which we often mistakenly label as mere "pests"—play a key role in maintaining the natural balance.

Ants are social insects, working together to build intricate colonies, transport huge volumes of material in orderly columns, and divide tasks among designated workers. But what is equally interesting about ants is how frequently they form symbiotic relationships with other species.

Some of North America's ant species form mutualisms with other insects. Honeypot ants, which live in desert and semi-desert regions as well as here in New England, herd aphids and other scale insects, bringing them under cover or into their own anthills at any sign of threat from predators. In our neck of the woods, the ants actually take their aphid cattle underground in the fall to protect them from the cold, carrying them back up to the surface when plants grow again in the spring.

The ants go to all this trouble because the aphids, unable to digest all of the sugar in the sap that they suck from leaves, excrete it as a sweet honeydew from their anuses. The ants expertly milk them for this honeydew by stroking the aphids' backs with their antennae. The honeydew provides a constant supply of food for the ants, and the ants provide protection and security for the aphids.

Yet another example of ants acting mutually with flowers takes place in the springtime, as our woods are bursting with wildflowers. Bloodroot, violets, trillium, hepatica, and other spring wildflowers depend on the eating habits of several local ant species to ensure their propagation. Each tiny seed from these plants comes equipped with a lipid-rich packet in the membrane of the outer seed coat called an eliasome, which is the perfect fatty food source for an ant. Biologists have been hard-pressed to find any important physiological use of the eliasome's contents by the plants themselves. Instead, they believe the eliasomes have evolved specifically as a food source to attract ants.

Look carefully and you may be able to see ants trucking these self-con-

tained sacs of food—seed still conveniently attached—across the forest floor and hiding them in underground caches. Once the ant has removed and eaten the stored fats, the fertile seed is discarded, having been successfully dispersed to a new habitat and buried carefully in the ground, ready to sprout the following spring. The wildflowers' mutualism with ants is crucial for seed dispersal throughout the forest.

Creeping, scurrying, and winding their way across the forest and garden floors, our local ants often go unnoticed and unacclaimed. But in many ways, these small workers are tying ecosystems together, connecting insects to plants, and creating delicately balanced mutual relationships of extreme importance to the workings of the whole system. Ants even form a mutual relationship of sorts with humans—cleaning up our favorite picnic spots so the ground will be clean and ready the next time we happen by. All in exchange for a few free crumbs. ⌒⌣

Local Forests, Local Lumber

Stephen Long

A generation or two ago, buying locally was the only option. Before the interstate system and shopping malls, and way before 800 numbers and Amazon.com, the goods that people needed in their daily lives were available within their communities. The trip to the store brought people into regular contact with their neighbors, and commerce helped to knit the community together.

One necessity that's still readily available from local producers but often overlooked is lumber. It's a good bet that within 20 miles of your house, you can find a sawmill selling construction lumber that will not only fit your needs but also be reasonably priced. The wood comes from forests across town, not from across the continent, and the money you pay for it will stay in the community longer since it, in turn, will pay wages to the sawmill crew or buy logs from a local logger who in turn pays the landowner for his trees.

In contrast, any lumber you buy at the lumberyard at building-supply stores will likely be Douglas fir trucked in from the Pacific Northwest or British Columbia, or Southern yellow pine from the Southeast. In either case, much of the price you pay is for trucking it thousands of miles. The one exception for finished lumber is if you're buying white pine boards for flooring or trim. Chances are good that white pine purchased anywhere in the region comes from northeastern forests.

Whether your project is a window box or a two-car garage, you can buy all the wood you need directly from the sawmill. The lumber direct from the mill will be rough; it will not have been planed smooth. It will be either air-dried or still green. On the other hand, when you go to the lumberyard, you'll always find dressed lumber that's been kiln-dried and surfaced on a planer. A dressed 2 x 4 measures 1½ inches thick by 3½ inches wide.

Most rough lumber goes for barns, sheds, and garages—nondwelling spaces that aren't going to be finished with drywall. But many builders wouldn't hesitate to frame a house in rough lumber, as long as it's uniformly dry.

Where do you find rough lumber? Most of these sawmills have been in business so long that word of mouth is all that's necessary to keep a steady stream of customers driving into the yard. Ask around: any carpenter, logger, or anybody else who works or plays with wood will be able to direct you to the nearest sawmill.

You're most likely to find hemlock or white pine, since that's what grows locally. Hemlock is the heaviest and the most rugged of the softwoods, while white pine is the most versatile. Perfectly acceptable as framing lumber, pine is beautiful when finished for trim, flooring, and even furniture.

At these local mills, you'll pay less for good-quality lumber, and you'll get a firsthand look at how your neighbors make a living. You'll see that, besides selling lumber, the owner has markets for the byproducts as well: sawdust goes to farmers for bedding, slabs are chipped for fuel or go to maple syrup producers to fire the sugarmaking arch, and bark is sold for landscaping mulch. These sawyers are truly a linchpin of the local economy.

Though many of the old-time rotary mills have closed their doors in recent years, springing up to replace them and filling the same niche is a new breed of sawmill, the portable bandsaw. Developed over the last 20 years, these mills have the advantage of a thinner saw kerf, so that more wood ends up as lumber and less as sawdust. And they are easier to maintain.

Many thousands of these mills have been sold in the last two decades. Some sawyers continue to operate them as portables, towing them onto a log landing and sawing the customer's logs on-site to the specifications they require. Others set up a permanent home for the mill, selling lumber to drive-in customers the way the rotary mills do. You'll locate these sawyers the same way: just ask around.

Buying local lumber helps accomplish the important ecological goal of keeping land forested and not developed. With high property taxes and higher prices for developable land, there is considerable pressure on landowners to sell or subdivide their forestland. Fragmentation of habitat is one of the biggest problems facing many wildlife species today. But when landowners are able to sell wood for lumber, they have an incentive to continue growing trees. Whether your primary pleasure in the woods is from bird watching, deer hunting, maple sugaring, snowmobiling, hiking, skiing, or simply watching the foliage, local lumber means local forests, and local forests are good news for everyone. ᘓ

Look, Fireflies!

Virginia Barlow

Deep down, most of us know that fireflies have a life, but a good firefly night brings such a flood of amazement and gratitude that questions about their larval phase, their diet, and their day jobs get crowded out. And what *are* they doing out there? Nearly all the flashes you see are emitted by males searching for females. The females have climbed blades of grass to join us in watching the luminous display.

In 1911, Frank McDermott, an amateur entomologist, discovered that more than one species of firefly was flashing in the meadow he was watching and that each had its own distinct flashing pattern, which he recorded. Jim Lloyd, who is carrying on the work of matching flash pattern to flasher, estimates that he has spent the equivalent of six years at night in the field tracking down little lights and catching and identifying the signalers—nowadays, needless to say, with more and more equipment.

However, according to Lloyd, anyone with a small, cheap penlight who knows the correct female response to a male firefly's flash pattern can step into a field of fireflies and soon have a male eagerly exploring the penlight with its antennae.

All 22 or so New England species are kept from breeding with different species by habitat, the time of day when they are active, flash color, and, most importantly, by flash pattern. It's a nifty little arrangement that can be studied just by watching. The love lives of most insects are conducted by pheromones—airborne chemical signals that draw males and females together—that remain undetected by us.

Precision on the penlight switch is important. The duration, color, and brightness of a flash response, and the time delay following the male's signal are all critical. You may need some practice with your penlight. It should be faced right into the ground; otherwise it is too bright.

But don't distract any one firefly for too long because their time is precious. The adults typically live for less than a week and search for mates for a limited period in the evening. Some begin flashing at dusk and have extinguished their lanterns soon after dark. Others get going only when it is quite dark, and these late risers may continue well into the night. When cruising, males are exposed to predators, so attempts to mate with the wrong species could cost more than a few wasted minutes. Except for some special cases, which we will get to in a minute, the female responds only to a male of her own species.

Take *Photinus marginellus*, the northern twilight firefly, for example. Common over lawns and the forest floor, the male flies about four feet above the ground and flashes a single yellow light, ¼-second long, every 3 seconds. The female flashes back from her perch on a blade of grass. The male may dim his light as he approaches, so as not to attract other males to his find. Mating occurs within a minute or so.

Pyractomena angulata (like most fireflies, it has no common name), on the other hand, frequents bushes and trees near marshes, and its eight amber flashes take place in about ¾ of a second and are repeated every 3 seconds. The female responds one-half second later with a single flash. (These times are correct when the temperature is at about 70° Fahrenheit. Flashing speeds up at higher temperatures.)

Too magical to be true? Well, yes. In fact, it gets downright gruesome. In the middle of this happy scene, you may find a firefly in the genus *Photuris*—perhaps *Photuris pennsylvanicus*, a common species (perhaps a group of species) in New England. Females in this genus have cracked the code of several *Photinus* species. With perfect timing, they flash an imitation of a *Photinus* female and lure in the eager *Photinus* male. The larger, longer legged, and more agile *Photuris* female then eats the unsuspecting suitor.

Imagine the effect this might have on the behavior of the firefly species that are being eaten. It's hard times for the prey species, but a boon to biologists who study how the behavior of one species af-

fects another. Have "dark fireflies"—daytime flying species that have lost the ability to flash and have gone back to using pheromones to find a mate—evolved in response to *Photuris's* deadly appetite? Have the *Photinus* females, who give two short flashes instead of one in response to a male's advertisement, found a way to keep their mates from the deadly lure of the *Photuris* femme fatales? ∾

Know When to Mow

Chuck Wooster

Hey—don't mow that field just yet! As dairy farms continue yielding to house lots, more and more of us find ourselves in possession of old hayfields and pastures. Since these open spaces are such beautiful parts of the landscape, many people want to keep them open. This, in turn, means that the fields need to be mowed regularly to keep the forest at bay. If you are lucky enough to own a hayfield or pasture, and growing grass isn't central to your economic livelihood, consider letting your field grow tall this summer and not cutting it until August or September.

Waiting until then will make a big difference to local wildlife.

Take the red-winged blackbird, for example, whose welcomed song on March mornings is among the first harbingers of spring. One of the redwing's preferred nesting sites is the tall grass of fields near wet areas, where a pair may raise as many as three broods per year between late April and mid-July. Cutting the hay during this time period not only eliminates the redwing's habitat but also can crush any eggs or chicks hiding in the grass.

The situation is even more critical for the bobolink, which nests exclusively in fields and pastures. Unlike the red-winged blackbird,

the bobolink typically has only one brood per year, making a tractor incursion during nesting season all the more devastating. Bobolink fledglings are likely to be hidden in the hay until as late as the Fourth of July. The eastern meadowlark, the upland sandpiper, and the field, savannah, grasshopper, and vesper sparrows all have similar nesting requirements.

Whitetail does often utilize the protection of tall grass to stash a fawn or two in the early weeks of June. Fawns during the first few weeks of their lives have no scent. Several acres of tall hay, therefore, make a great hiding place where a fawn can gain strength out of sight of calculating coyote eyes.

And then there are the bugs and insects that rely on tall grasses and flowering weeds. Some of these are as beloved as the firefly, whose June numbers are much greater over uncut fields than over cut ones, or as terrifying as the ambush bug, which waits under the flowers of boneset and milkweed in August to attack and devour unsuspecting bees. Though these insects aren't as charismatic as spotted fawns or baby chicks, they're still an integral part of the larger ecosystem.

All of which is to say, if you have a choice about when to mow your field or pasture, choose later rather than sooner. You'll still have the beauty of land kept open for future years, and the birds and bees will have the benefit of tall-grass habitat during the prime summer season.

Of course, you can also mow your field only every third year or so. In addition to saving the time, expense, and fuel required for annual mowing, you will be creating a habitat where brush intermingles with grass—even better for bobolink, and not bad for woodcock or possibly cottontails. If raspberries spring up, so will bears and other animals who feast on berries. Don't try this three-year approach, however, if you have plans to bring the field back into hay at some point—it's a major operation to return raspberry thickets to grasses and clover.

And don't pull your local dairy farmer down from the tractor to confront him or her with this article. Cutting hay in June may be terrible for an individual bobolink but is of great benefit to bobolinks overall. The patchwork pattern of corn fields, hay fields, heifer pastures, and open space that makes for such great wildlife habitat is a direct result of our dairy farming economy. As long as dairy farming remains viable in Vermont and New Hampshire, we will always benefit from the diversity of wildlife habitat that dairying creates. If we stopped cutting hay and let all our pastures revert to forest, the bobolink

and meadowlark would escape the cutter bar only to find that the old neighborhood had grown in.

For dairy farmers, cutting hay in June captures the nutrition of the first flush of spring grass and sets the stage for a second or third cutting of hay later in the summer. If dairy farmers weren't out right now cutting hay, it would make matters worse for yet another critter that's becoming increasingly rare in northern New England these days: the dairy cow. ✐

A Mouth and Stomach on Legs

Ted Levin

One summer night, in the light of a half moon, I saw a bullfrog trespass on another's territory. The owner met the challenge full force. Eight times he inflated his lungs and guts, then leaped in the air, erect and bloated. A jolly shoving match ensued, with both squat frogs bouncing and grappling like sumo wrestlers. To the victor—in this case the larger frog and resident landowner—went the spoils: the more prominent calling site.

Sometimes, if the losing male is small and careless, he may himself become part of the spoils and wind up in the belly of his assailant.

A female bullfrog must be equally careful when selecting a mate. If she chooses a male that exceeds her size (bullfrogs may grow to be eight inches from nose to vent), she may end up defending herself rather than mating. The prudent female gauges the size of her suitor by the depth and resonance of his voice, approaching only those males whose dimensions seem compatible with her own.

The wetland near our house, which exceeds 70 acres in size, supports perhaps a dozen calling males. They begin their serenade in late afternoon, when the water temperature is close to 70° Fahrenheit, and continue calling throughout the night. Each *jug-o-rum* of the bullfrog carries more than a quarter mile. But for all their power and aggression, bullfrogs are cautious beasts; when I'm observing them, they always wait for me to stop moving before rebroadcasting their intentions.

Bullfrogs attach their eggs to submerged vegetation in June and July. Because the water is warm, embryonic development is quick, and the tadpoles hatch in less than two weeks. By the time bullfrog eggs hatch, spring peepers have long since left the water to join wood frogs on the forest floor, gray treefrogs have returned to the trees, and American toads are back in the garden.

The tadpoles of bullfrogs, which grow to more than six inches in length, may take three summers to develop into froglets. When metamorphosis is complete, herds of these small bullfrogs station themselves along the shoreline and wait for unsuspecting aquatic insects—dragonflies, mayflies, water striders, water boatmen—while attempting to avoid the cavernous mouths of their parents.

Of all our local amphibians, the adult bullfrog has the most varied diet. Any animal that can fit into its mouth is suitable food. So great is its appetite that a bullfrog can be thought of as a mouth and stomach propelled by huge hind legs. I have dissected bullfrogs and found their stomachs crammed with baby painted and snapping turtles, crayfish, dragonflies, and other frogs. It makes no difference whether it's a wood frog or peeper, American toad or gray treefrog, or even a newly minted bullfrog; if it moves and if it's small enough, it's eaten.

I once watched a moderately sized bullfrog stuff a full-grown green frog in its mouth. For ten minutes, the green frog struggled, its feet flailing from the bigger frog's mouth, until, tired and deprived of air, it relaxed, disappearing down the cavernous void. As soon as the bullfrog forced down its lunch, it stationed itself by the shoreline and waited for another victim.

Even barn swallows and cliff swallows, which go to the shore to collect mud for their nests, and swamp sparrows, which stalk through the reeds, may wind up in the belly of a bullfrog. Unsuspecting hummingbirds sipping nectar from blossoms of jewelweed and cardinal flower are caught; so are meadow voles, water shrews, ducklings, and mid-sized snakes.

I know of no other animal whose voice, relative to its size, projects as far as that of the bullfrog's. Many years ago, I lived in a cottage next to a small millpond that was full of bullfrogs. Every evening the males climbed up on small boulders that were scattered around the shallows, one frog to a rock, and filled the night with their deep calls. From a distance they sounded like a roll of thunder, it was so deafening.

But I was not the only one tuned to their clamor. A pair of barred owls regularly perched on snags and hunted the frogs. In the morning, a red-shouldered hawk took over. A family of raccoons and an itinerant otter also used the pond as their larder and drove the frogs, leaping and squealing with terror, into the depths of the pond. American bitterns and mink also take their share of bullfrog tadpoles and froglets.

In the case of the resident bully, the turnabout somehow seems justified. ∽

Queen for a Summer

Catherine Tudish

A couple of summers ago, while working in my garden and enjoying the company of bumblebees buzzing in the tall, ferny asparagus, I noticed something strange. Each of the bees appeared to have a small orange nodule stuck to its thigh. Was this a new species of bee? Was something wrong?

Soon after, an amused naturalist friend set me straight. They were normal worker bees out foraging, collecting pollen in the pollen baskets on their rear legs. Only because asparagus pollen is bright orange had I finally seen it, but every bumblebee out and about in midsummer is carrying a load of pollen, usually in more subdued shades.

When a worker bee—an infertile female—enters a flower to sip nectar with her long tongue, the thick hair of her body also picks up pollen grains. Using the "combs and brushes" (patches of shorter, coarser hairs on the insides of her hind legs), she gathers up this pollen and puts it into the baskets—smooth areas on the upper legs surrounded by spiky hairs. At the same time, she is storing nectar in the honeycrop, a flexible sac in her abdomen. Unlike some other bees, which forage for nectar and pollen on separate trips, a bumblebee generally gathers both at once. The nectar is the colony's essential energy source while the pollen contains the protein needed for the queen to produce more eggs and to feed the larvae and newly hatched bees.

A foraging trip can take an individual bee as far as two miles from her nest. On her return, she regurgitates the nectar into wax honeypots and transfers the pollen to a storage vessel, often a recycled cocoon, by rubbing her back legs together. The food is consumed by the queen, larvae, and "house" bees, the small workers that remain in the nest to care for the young, carry out debris, and stand guard. Developing from egg to larva to adult bee in 16–25 days, a worker begins to forage within a few days and then lives only about two more weeks.

A bumblebee colony begins anew each spring when a single queen emerges from hibernation in an underground burrow. After feeding on the nectar and pollen of early-flowering plants, she begins searching for a nest site. Having been inseminated the previous fall, the queen also begins to produce eggs, which she will lay once she finds the right spot—possibly the abandoned nest of a mouse, vole, or chipmunk, within which she creates a small cavity by pulling dried grass in close to her body.

Here, the queen fashions a tiny honeypot from wax scales exuded from glands between the segments of her abdomen and fills it with nectar. After building up a store of pollen, some of which she forms into a ball moistened with nectar (called "bee bread"), she lays her first batch of 8–10 eggs on the pollen ball and covers it with wax. The queen spends a lot of time sitting on this brood clump and feeding from the nearby honeypot, but she also makes frequent foraging trips. When the larvae hatch, they spin cocoons of silk and pupate inside them. The original brood clump continues to grow as the queen adds new egg packets and new larvae build their cocoons.

Once the first brood of workers has emerged, the queen stays inside the nest, producing more eggs and caring for the young. A bumblebee colony eventually becomes an interconnected jumble of egg packets, larval cocoons, honeypots, and old cocoons used for storage. The ultimate size of a colony depends on the particular species and the food supply. Some have as few as 30 bees, while the largest might have 400. Bumblebees have few predators, though skunks and shrikes will invade a nest for the honey and don't seem to mind getting stung.

As fall approaches in northern New England, the bumblebee colony begins to change. For the first time, males (or drones), which grow from unfertilized eggs, and queens emerge, and the colony produces no more workers. Males leave the nest after a few days and fend for themselves, but they remain nearby to mate with the new queens, who eat a lot of nectar and fill their honeycrops in preparation for hibernation. By the time winter arrives, the old queen, any remaining workers, and the males have died off.

In Vermont and New Hampshire, as elsewhere, wild honeybees have been decimated by mites and other pests, and even the hardy bumblebee is threatened by insecticides and loss of natural food sources. A few small steps, such as not using poisonous chemicals in our yards and gardens and growing plants bees love, can help enormously. Bumblebees are drawn to purple, blue, white, and yellow flowers, such as lupines, joe-pye weed, blueberry, sunflowers, monkshood, asters, and goldenrod. And, of course, asparagus. ∾

July

❧

FIRST WEEK

1

Roadsides are looking good if they are lined
by Queen Anne's lace and chicory.

Female eastern milk snakes lay about
a dozen eggs in July. They will
hatch in six to eight weeks.

The fragrance of milkweed in bloom
can be almost overwhelming. Bees,
moths, wasps, butterflies, and even
flies are drawn to its nectar.

Wild leek leaves have faded away. The white, star-
like flowers are out now, in a cluster on a single stalk.

Honeybee lore: A swarm in July isn't worth a fly.

SECOND WEEK

2

Willow cone galls reach full size. Resembling
pinecones, each gall began in late April when a
small fly laid an egg in a willow terminal bud.

Yarrow blooms all summer long. The leaves
can be chewed to relieve toothache.

Wild turkey hens and their poults may join
others to form family flocks of 30 or more birds.

Little brown bats may consume half
their weight in insects in an evening.
Look for them over wetlands or still
water, where insects are most abundant.

THIRD WEEK

3

Tall meadow rue is blooming, its feathery flower heads well above other roadside and marshy plants.

Hummingbird foreheads are pollinating cardinal flowers. Their bills are licking nectar from deep within the flower.

Look for anglewings. Most of these butterflies, in the genus Polygonia, live in the forest and look like dead leaves.

Crickets begin singing.

At about one-half inch long, spring peepers will transform into adults and take up a terrestrial existence.

FOURTH WEEK

4

Virgin's bower, a high-climbing vine of moist areas, is flowering. Its even showier, plumed fruits will appear later.

Flickers on the ground are probably eating ants. They eat more ants than any other North American bird.

Wood turtles eat lots of mushrooms in July and August.

If eastern chipmunks produce two litters, the second batch is usually born in late July.

Blueberries are in fruit. Cedar waxwings will pass the berries one to another until each has been fed.

Healthy Forests?

Virginia Barlow

What makes a forest healthy? And can logging improve forest health? Perhaps you've seen ads—from paper companies, loggers, and sometimes foresters—with this message: "If you want your forest to be healthy, call us today!" It's a very tempting invitation, for above all else, we all want healthy forests. But can logging really improve the health of a forest?

The answer is an emphatic maybe. There are many good reasons to cut trees in your woods, but improving forest health is, at best, questionable.

First there's the question, what is a healthy forest? It's not a green dreamland where nothing dies. On the contrary, it is a place where everything dies. Trees, especially, are killers. New young ones fight each other to the death, shading out their neighbors as they reach for the sun. By the time a tree has reached the canopy, it has killed dozens of its compatriots.

A multitude of organisms has evolved to capture the enormous amount of energy that is stored in dead trees of all sizes. Some of these organisms have figured out how to feed not just on dead, but on dying trees. And, yes, some insects, bacteria, and fungi jump the gun a little and kill stressed trees.

But notice that these agents of death are themselves forms of life. They actively recycle leaves, bark, and wood, keeping a grip on most of the nutrients until another living plant can incorporate them once again. The rate at which trees grow is closely coupled to the rate at which animals and microbes consume dead plants, releasing essential nutrients for tree uptake. In a healthy forest, predators, weather, and the trees' chemical defenses combine to keep insects and diseases below the levels that seriously harm the plant community. Individual trees die; the plant community lives.

If death doesn't signify ill health, what does? And can a logging job fix it? Seriously ill forests are missing whole generations of trees or important tree species. Pollution is thought to be the main cause of the terribly sick forests in Europe. And we all know about the losses in this country from introduced diseases and insects; I won't repeat the long, all too familiar, sorrowful list. Whether it's the "cogs in the wheel" or "rivets in the airplane" analogy of ecological health, losing key pieces is not good for the community. Logging, however, can't cure these problems and didn't cause them.

What logging can do is to greatly improve a forest's productivity. Even if you yourself have never marked the trees to be removed in a logging operation, you can imagine what it's like: freeing some of the best trees to grow, removing some of those that are poorly formed, suppressed, or diseased. Working carefully over a long period of time, landowners and foresters can dramatically change a forest's ultimate value and usefulness to humans, while preserving almost all of its beauty and ecological integrity.

There is no way logging could improve the health of a pristine, untouched forest, especially one magically isolated from today's polluted air. But most of the forest now growing in the Northeast is far from untouched. Instead, our woods usually consist of trees of the same age—even-aged stands—that became established on abandoned fields and pastures. This situation is unnatural enough that a thoughtful logging operation has a good chance of making it better. Harvests that result in sunny openings, for instance, provide enough sunlight for seedlings and saplings to become established, and a new generation of trees is able to get a start. This adds complexity and creates what foresters and ecologists call structural diversity, a plus for many wildlife species.

I'd love to think that logging can cure a forest's ills, but it seems to me that logging, for the most part, is exactly like everything else we humans do—whether it's driving a car, eating a

meal, or reading a newspaper: our every move takes some small something from the earth and diverts it to our species. None of us is a hero in Mother Nature's eyes. The best we can do is to minimize our impact. Cutting trees for our needs close to home, using methods that are in harmony with nature and which sustain the health and diversity of the forest, easily beats most of the alternatives. ∾

The Eel Deal

Madeline Bodin

Right this minute, in the Connecticut River, is a very large, old eel. She has a snakelike body (yet she is a fish, with fins) and is a greenish-brownish color. She is slimy and will get even slimier if she winds up on your fishhook. She has traveled far, and before her life is over, she will retrace her journey back to the middle of the Atlantic Ocean. That is, if she is not pureed in the turbines of a hydroelectric dam on her way downstream (as were up to 37 percent of the eels in a recent American study).

I must confess, I haven't seen this particular eel myself. I'm relying on the calendar and statistics to know she is there. First, eels are active at night, and I am not. Second, I was counting on the Bellows Falls Fish Ladder to give me an underwater window to the river, but the ladder won't be filled with water until an Atlantic salmon is spotted at the Vernon dam in southern Vermont, which hadn't typically happened as of mid-June.

But the calendar and the statistics tell me she is there, somewhere. The calendar says summer, and while the water is warm, eels that are moving are moving upstream. The statistics say that nearly all of the eels found in Vermont and New Hampshire are female. The statistics also say that female eels may be 5 feet long and may live 20 years or more. The males tend to stay in estuaries, the areas where rivers and oceans meet and mix. They grow to about two feet long.

Before dams were built, American eels (there is just one species in the eastern U.S.) were found everywhere in the Connecticut River and its tributaries. A biography of George Perkins Marsh, a Vermonter sometimes called the first environmentalist, describes him catching eels in the White River when he began attending school in Royalton in 1811.

Dams reduced the number of eels in the upper Connecticut but did not eliminate them. "I've seen them climbing up a vertical concrete wall when they are small," says Alex Haro, ecologist with the Silvio O. Conte Anadromous Fish Research Lab in Turners Falls, Massachusetts, and a leading eel researcher. When dams added fishways in the 1980s, and rock-climbing skills were no longer mandatory for eel survival, the number of eels in the upper Connecticut increased. "Compared to climbing over the dam, it's easier," Haro says of the fish ladders.

Ironically, even as we see more eels in Vermont and New Hampshire, the American eel population as a whole appears to be declining, Haro says. It's hard to find historical records of eel populations over long periods, but the available records show eel numbers going down.

The eels swimming right now in the Connecticut River were hatched in the Sargasso Sea, the part of the Atlantic Ocean roughly between Bermuda and the Azores Islands, which is the calm center in the middle of the Atlantic held in place by swirling oceanic currents. The eels first floated around as plankton for up to a year. Then, as 2-inch-long, transparent "glass eels," they found their way to Long Island Sound while their kin wound up in estuaries from Canada to South America. In Long Island Sound, they became pigmented and were then called "elvers."

Slightly older and slightly larger "yellow eels" (actually that greenish or yellowish brown color) act like preschoolers on a playground: the girls go one way and the boys go another. While the male eels tend to stay in the estuary (as on the playground, there are exceptions), the females tend to head upstream.

Haro says they will keep heading upstream every late spring, summer, and early fall for the next five to seven years. "Once they reach a certain age and size," he says, "they settle down and set up a territory."

Our eel will live in her territory for up to 15 more years. Then, one fall, she will turn a silver-gray color, stop eating, and start downstream. If this sounds a lot like a salmon, it is, except it is backward. While salmon, shad, and alewives are anadromous, returning to rivers to spawn, eels are catadromous, returning to the ocean to spawn.

With luck, she'll make it back to the Sargasso Sea, where males and females from all over the western Atlantic will meet for a kind of eel spring break. After what I can only imagine as an all-too-brief orgy (I say brief because it's the only sex they will have in their lives and because they all die when it's over), the cycle begins again. ∾

Ecological Lawn Care

Anne Margolis

There is a crop that most of us spend many hours on in the summer. We don't eat it, sell it, or put it in vases, but most of us couldn't image living without it. It is grass.

Somewhere along the way, we become imprinted with the image of the "perfect lawn." Golf courses occupy the extreme end of the spectrum; most of us are happy with a lawn that is lush and healthy. For some, that means applying products to erase pests and uninvited plants. Such care creates the perfect canvas for a Saturday mowing.

But what about that mowing? The 54 million people in the U.S. who regularly mow their 30 million acres of lawn consume 800 million gallons of gasoline a year and account for more than 5 percent of urban air pollution, according to the Environmental Protection Agency. And we collectively apply 70 million pounds of pesticides to our yards, more than 10 times per acre what farmers use.

But pesticides and fertilizers don't necessarily stay within the lawn's bounds. The newly formed Vermont Green Lawn Coalition is trying to get the word out that healthy soil and clean water are inextricably linked. The lawn fertilizers and pesticides we apply can inadvertently travel throughout our watersheds, and while they may make a lawn look good for awhile, they can be detrimental in the long term.

According to Paul Sachs, owner of an ecological lawn-care company called North Country Organics in Bradford, Vermont, if you don't have the soil functioning properly, you have to keep grass alive chemically, much like keeping somebody alive in a hospital. "Soil is the plants' digestive and immune systems," he says. "If you don't have a healthy soil, you're constantly battling things with chemical suppressants. The more you use them, the more you need to use them."

These chemicals strip the soil of the very elements it needs to stay healthy: the humus, fungi, bacteria, protozoa, and microbes working to break down rock into nutrients and keep the soil structured, with places for grass roots to grow and water to percolate. Just as farmers incorporate compost to build their soil structure, we "grass gardeners" need to address the "root of the problem," so to speak: our soil health.

So how to start? Sachs recommends the screwdriver test. You should be able to drive the shaft of a 6- or 8-inch screwdriver into the turf with little effort. "If you can't get it in more than an inch without straining, your soil is severely compacted," says Sachs. "No amount of fertilizer or lime will fix it." For mild compaction, application of well-composted material will enhance soil structure. For severe compaction, mechanical aeration of the turf is called for.

Sachs also recommends conducting a soil test, which can be done through the University of Vermont or the New Hampshire Cooperative Extension. Your soil's pH should be anywhere from 6.0 to 7.5. If it isn't, Sachs suggests some sort of fertility to feed soil organisms—organic fertilizer is good; mature compost is even better, especially if the ingredients are naturally derived. Your goal is to feed the soil, not the grass.

A lawn with healthy soil, to which some compost and some organic fertilizer is added, will mostly take care of itself. You can deturf and reseed a really patchy lawn with a native Northeast grass mix or even a perennial groundcover that doesn't have to be mowed. Maybe dandelions aren't so bad; at least they attract pollinators to our yards, where they might visit an apple blossom or two.

Most importantly, while short lawns are nice and neat to look at, they're also hard on the grass itself. If you keep the mower deck raised to at least 3 inches off the ground, your grass will be much hardier. It will stand up nicely to heat and dry spells, be less susceptible to most pest problems, and you won't have to mow as often.

What about problems when they do occur? Dog-pee spots are caused by an overabundance of nitrogen. A little extra water will help flush the nitrogen more quickly. You can apply milky spore bacterium or beneficial nematodes to eliminate grubs, says Sachs, products that are available in garden stores and catalogs. When grubs leave, skunks and moles leave, too. Finally, bare patches can be covered with a layer of compost and reseeded.

With all the free time you'll gain and money you'll save by managing your lawn in an ecologically thoughtful way, you can enjoy your grass crop, knowing you won't be contributing to the extra consumption of oil or the degradation of our air and waterways through excess fertilizer and pesticides. Your kids and pets will be safe from chemicals, and you will have the best-looking lawn in the neighborhood. ❧

In the Great Blue Heronry

~

Madeline Bodin

We could hear the pond before we could see it. The shrill *oak-a-ree* of red-winged blackbirds could be heard well into the surrounding forest. Closer to the pond, the loose banjo-string call of a green frog joined in. A few steps later we heard the bullfrogs, sounding like a jug-band chorus.

The adult herons flew off the moment Wally Elton, our group's leader, stepped into the clearing. When I entered, the first thing I noticed were two heron fledglings standing tall in their nest of sticks built on a spindly human-made tripod in the middle of a long-abandoned beaver pond. The fledglings were about two and a half feet tall, and their grayish feathers matched the weathered wood of the tripod and their stick nest.

Great blue herons are big birds. The adults can be over four feet tall and have a wingspan of nearly six feet. It makes sense that their fledglings are similarly large. Great blue herons prefer to breed in secluded wetlands, away from their usual feeding grounds, and they have found just such a place in Weathersfield, Vermont, in an old beaver pond surrounded by forest.

The Ascutney Mountain Audubon Society has had its eye on this place for about 15 years, monitoring the number of great blue heron nests and fledglings each year. The annual monitoring is what brought Elton (Ascutney Mountain Audubon's vice president), some of its board members, and me to the heronry—which is also called a heron rookery or colony.

In 1992 this heronry reached a peak of 12 nests, but the monitors noticed that the dead pines supporting the nests were beginning to fall. When the number of nests plummeted to six the next year, the Society took action. They worked with the Vermont Department of Fish and Wildlife to erect two tripods to provide alternative nest sites. In 2002, the year I visited the rookery, Elton counted 13 great blue heron fledglings in six nests built on four of the five tripods at the site. In 2001 there were five nests and 15 fledglings.

Great blue heron numbers declined severely in the 1960s and 1970s when DDT, a chemical intended to control mosquito larvae, caused the shells of heron eggs to thin and crack before the chicks were able to survive. With DDT now banned in the United States, herons are so numerous that there hasn't been an official study of heron breeding sites in Vermont in about 15 years, says Everett Marshall, a nongame biologist with the Vermont Department of Fish and Wildlife. Marshall suspects there may be as many as 100 heronries in Vermont.

The great blue heronries of New Hampshire have been studied in more depth and more recently. A 10-year study by the Audubon Society of New Hampshire was completed in 1992, when there were 123 active heronries. The time-consuming and difficult-to-fund study ended, explains Chris Martin, senior biologist with the Audubon Society of New Hampshire, when it became clear that the heron population was quite stable.

While the number of nests and fledglings in the Weathersfield heronry varies little, the beaver pond itself is decisively changing from pond to marsh. Elton pointed out that one of the tripods is now on dry ground and is unattractive as a heron nesting site because predators have an easier time accessing the nests.

While heronries are found in several kinds of wetlands, Martin said that herons have a special—if temporary—relationship with beaver ponds containing standing dead trees. "The problem is, these trees decay over time," Martin said. "The beavers abandon the pond, the pond dries out, and it's not useful to the herons anymore." This is exactly what is happening in Weathersfield.

The herons, though, don't seem to have a problem moving around the landscape, following the beavers.

Martin feels that as long as beavers are still out there, the herons will have a place to breed.

Meanwhile, osprey are following the herons. New England's osprey population was also hit hard during the DDT years and is still recovering. In the last few years, more than half of the 15 or 20 new nesting pairs of ospreys found in southern New Hampshire have been in heronries. Though osprey and herons both eat fish (herons eat frogs, reptiles, and small mammals, too), the two species coexist peacefully, perhaps because both travel away from the nesting area to get food for themselves and their young.

At the time of my visit, ospreys weren't nesting in the Weathersfield heronry, although the unused platform-on-a-pole provides just the kind of nesting site they might like. But the herons had the frogs and the blackbirds for company, as well as cattails, blue flag iris, and ferns as the pond dries out. As our group prepared to leave the heronry, a swarm of electric-blue damselflies flitted over the ferns, and the jug band chorus started up again. ∽

An Archipelago of Summits

Steve Faccio

Just for a moment, imagine what the Northeast would look like if seas were to rise 4,000 feet higher than they are now. Northern New England would be reduced to a series of islands—an archipelago of summits. You could surf cast for striped bass from the summit of New Hampshire's Mount Tecumseh or stroll among tidal pools on the flanks of Camel's Hump in Vermont.

Yet, even without this drastic flood, these "islands" still exist. But instead of being surrounded by salt water, they rise from a sea of woodlots, hayfields, and pastures, villages, small towns, and cities.

Ecologically, the region's high elevations are islands, providing unique habitats which, like traditional islands, are isolated from each other. These unique habitats are home to many species of plants and animals—even entire communities—that are rare in the region. Many of these species exist as so-called outlier populations, far removed from their main geographic ranges. Several appear on state and federal endangered species lists, and a few, like Bicknell's Thrush or Dwarf Cinquefoil, are endemic—existing nowhere else in the world.

How can you tell if you're atop one of these alpine islands? Most dramatically, there are no trees, except perhaps the occasional stunted conifer huddled in the lee of a boulder or ledge. Few plants grow taller than the cuff of an average hiking boot. The Presidential and Franconia Ranges in New Hampshire are the two largest "islands" in our local archipelago, though there are many smaller islets such as the summits of Mount Moosilauke and the Kinsmans in New Hampshire and the summits of Mansfield, Camel's Hump, and Killington in Vermont.

The first person to experience this unique alpine area and leave a written record of the event was an English settler named Darby Field. In 1642, along with two Native American companions, Field reached the summit of Mt. Washington. One hundred and thirty years later, in 1772, Ira Allen climbed Mt. Mansfield and surveyed that ridgeline. For early explorers, reaching these summits without the luxury of trails must have been a daunting effort, but it also subjected them to firsthand experience of the elevational changes that occur in plant communities.

As anyone who has spent time in the mountains knows, the closer you get to the clouds, the colder and wetter it gets. With every 1,000-foot increase in elevation, there is a corresponding drop of 3° Fahrenheit in average temperature and an increase of about 8 inches in average precipitation. This results in a shorter growing season with wetter, more acidic, and less fertile soils than in the lowlands. Not surprisingly, overall species diversity drops as elevation increases.

Once you reach treeline, you enter the wind-whipped world known as alpine tundra. In this fragile area, natural rock gardens consisting of dwarf shrubs (primarily heaths and willows), small patches of moss, lichen-covered rocks, clumps of sedges and rushes, and an amazing display of diminutive wildflowers form a mosaic of colors, patterns, and textures. Perennial plants, whose roots survive the winters to sprout again, are the rule in the alpine zone. Annuals—plants that complete their life cycle in one season, leaving only their seeds behind—have trouble competing in such a short growing season.

While alpine plants are hardy, most depend upon a blanket of insulating snow to protect them from winterkill. As many as 75 species of plants are restricted to the alpine zone and cannot be found growing at lower elevations unless you travel 1,000 miles north to the arctic tundra of Canada and Alaska. Indeed, nearly two-thirds of Mt. Washington's alpine plants exist as disjunct populations, or outliers, far removed from the heart of their geographic range.

The high elevations of New York, Vermont, New Hampshire, and Maine are special places, rich in biological treasures, geological history, and ecological significance. They are also attractive places,

both for the plants and animals that together make up the varied ecological communities and for human visitors. Who hasn't been inspired by the sight of a snow-swept Mt. Washington towering in the distance, or a sunset view of the Adirondacks rising beyond Lake Champlain, or the familiar silhouette of Camel's Hump looming above a spring morning's fog?

If you have an opportunity to visit our archipelago of summits this summer, keep an eye out for some of the unique wildflowers of our alpine tundra, such as diapensia, mountain sandwort, alpine bilberry, and moss campion. But remember to stay on the trail while you're up there. These tenacious plants, whose island homes are buffeted by hurricane-force winds dozens of times each year, are helpless beneath the tread of even a few stray footsteps. ∾

Don't Get Bogged Down!

Rose Paul

Some people call any wet, mucky place a bog, or maybe a swamp. They hardly ever think to call it a fen. It may well be a fen, of course, unless it's a marsh. Or possibly a seep.

How to sort all this out?

First, observe the water in the wetland. Is it flowing or stagnant? If it's flowing, you have yourself a marsh. Marshes usually occur adjacent to ponds, lakes, slow-moving rivers, or at river mouths. The constant movement of water increases the oxygen content in the water, brings an inflow of nutrients, and promotes decomposition. A fine, black muck soil develops that is high in well-decomposed organic matter. Various grasses and sedges thrive in marshes, including the familiar cattail. There are almost never any woody plants growing in a marsh because they cannot grow in standing water.

There is a second type of wetland that has flowing water in it, though compared to a marsh, it's usually very small: a seep. The flowing water in a seep comes from underground, where cracks in the bedrock direct flow toward the surface. Seeps can persist throughout the year and often form the headwaters of perennial streams. One feature of a seep is the constant temperature of the groundwater year-round. This allows vegetation such as grasses and sedges to get an early start in the spring, providing food for animals such as bears and deer.

If the water in your wetland is not flowing, then you don't have a marsh or a seep, and you need to ask yourself a second question: are there woody plants growing in it? If there are, then you're talking about a swamp. Swamps always occur in low spots in the forest that have wet soils, but not so wet that woody plants are excluded. They are only intermittently wet, during spring flooding and heavy summer storms. Swamps can be small dips in the landscape, taking up an acre or so, or they can occupy many hundreds of acres. Trees such as black ash, green ash, red maple, and swamp white oak are well adapted to the seasonally wet conditions of swamps.

If your stagnant-water wetland has few or no trees growing in it, then you're left with one of three possible choices: a bog, a fen, or a vernal pool. The vernal pool is the easiest to identify because it's small and only seasonally wet. Essentially, it is a swamp without trees. Vernal pools are lined with bedrock or dense gravel called hardpan that can hold water well into the summer months. They typically lack inlets and outlets, gathering water from snowmelt and rainfall. In the spring they teem with amphibian life. Frogs and salamanders depend on them for breeding, egg-laying, and larval development. Because they dry out each year, vernal pools lack predators, such as small fish, that would normally prey on such a bounty of food.

Finally, if your wetland is wet all year, has stagnant water with no perceptible flow, and has few or no trees growing in it, you're down to two options: a bog or a fen. Bogs are the most nutrient-poor of the wetlands. With little to no inflow or outflow, decomposition happens slowly, acids build up, and nutrients are scarce. Most of the water and minerals in a bog come from rainfall and airborne dust. Bog plants have developed creative ways to absorb nutrients. For instance, acid-loving dwarf shrubs have partnerships with fungi in their roots that make soil nutrients more available, while carnivorous pitcher plants, sundews, and bladderworts go after their food more directly, trapping and dissolving little insects. The most abundant plants in a bog are sphagnum mosses and acid-loving dwarf shrubs called heaths, including cranberries, leatherleaf, Labrador tea, and bog laurel.

Life in the fen is much easier than in a bog. While the water in a fen appears to be stagnant, water does in fact flow, albeit slowly and imperceptibly, flushing out the acidic byproducts of decomposition. Fens are fed by an upwelling of groundwater that is laden with calcium and other minerals. A rich fen looks like a lush, wet grassland and is dominated by sedges. Rich fens have many more species of plants and different mosses than bogs. High spots called hummocks are home to some of our native wetland shrubs like alternate-leaved buckthorn, shrubby cinquefoil, and the white-leaved hoary willow.

New England's most famous fen was in Boston's Back Bay, near the aptly named Fenway Park. But be careful not to identify wetlands solely by their proper names. Eshqua Bog, for example, a much-visited wetland in Hartland, Vermont, that is well known for its showy lady's slipper orchids, is not a bog but a fen. It's just so tempting to call everything a bog! ∽

August

AUGUST

FIRST WEEK

1

Oak branches littering the ground may be the work
of the oak twig pruner. You can find the larva by
cutting open the end of the fallen branch.

Groups of whirligig beetles often swim
in circles. Each beetle has four eyes, two
looking up and two below the water line.

Large dragonflies such as the green darner may
replace flying with some gliding on hot days
to prevent overheating their flight muscles.

Katydids are in full chorus;
cicada calls are increasing.

SECOND WEEK

2

Goldenrods will be the most noticeable
flowers for the next month or so.

The first blackberries are ripe.

Splashes of red are starting to show here
and there on a few scattered red maples.

During the Dog Days, chipmunks stay below
ground and live on stored nuts and seeds.

Hermit thrushes have an extended breeding
season and will continue to sing long
after most other birds have fallen silent.

Male scarlet tanagers are looking strange
as they molt from red to green.

THIRD WEEK

New England asters starting to bloom.

Praise the redbelly snake, for slugs are a
big part of its diet. These snakes are now
giving birth to up to 21 live snakelets.

Newborn spiders, hanging from strands of
gossamer, may ride the winds for two weeks.

The messy nests of fall webworms are
beginning to be visible near the tips of
tree branches, especially along roads.

Last of snowshoe hare young are born. Females
may produce up to three litters, beginning in May.

FOURTH WEEK

Insect music replaces bird song, a sign of summer's end.

Clouds of pollen fill the air in cattail marshes.

All summer, aphids have been providing
ants with honeydew. Now ants are
carrying aphids underground to keep
them safe through the winter.

Woodchucks are fattening up for the
winter. Adults will consume up to one and
a half pounds of green vegetation a day.

Now a raven's diet will include corn, blackberries, and
other fruits. In winter, it's back to mostly carrion.

Ruffed Grouse Finds Its Way

Stephen Long

In the world of sporting literature, the ruffed grouse holds a position of respect that borders on awe. It is well known for its wariness, the explosiveness of its flush, and its capacity once airborne to take evasive action, maneuvering its way through a maze of tree limbs like a star halfback. Hunter or not, if you spend time in the woods, chances are you have been startled by the heart-stopping flush of this native of our thickets.

Can this awe-inspiring rocket possibly be the same mottled brown and gray bird that in the next couple of months you might see standing confused in the middle of the road wondering how it got there? The same bird that sometimes crashes into kitchen windows? Same species, yes. But the confused bird is most likely a juvenile of four or so months just embarking on its perilous dispersal from its natal flock. It's the size of an adult—at 17–25 ounces, it's bigger than a pigeon but slighter than most chickens—but it doesn't have an adult's experience. Out seeking its own territory, it literally doesn't know where it is. But before we join it on this trip, let's start with the egg.

Surviving in the egg long enough to hatch is itself an accomplishment, for it means that the nest has remained undiscovered for up to 40 days: two weeks or so while the 8 to 12 eggs are being laid, at the rate of one every day and a half, and an additional 24 to 26 days of incubation beneath the hen. The clutch of brown eggs sits on the ground in a nest that is little more than a hollowed-out depression in the leaf litter, often at the base of a tree or stump. The nest will be positioned so the hen can sense approaching predators, but it's no wonder that some nests are discovered and the eggs consumed by crows, ravens, weasels, and raccoons.

If they do hatch, grouse practically hit the ground running. Unlike most birds, grouse are ready to leave the nest as soon as they are dry. Insects provide an important source of protein as the chicks are feverishly working to develop muscles, bones, and feathers. If they come up against a stretch of cool, wet weather before their feathers have developed enough to offer some protection, the smallest chicks will not survive. The clutch of 12 could be reduced by a third within a couple of weeks.

Those that survive will be flying by the time they are five days old. Smaller than a humming-bird, they will take their first short flight, lighting on a branch in response to some danger.

Be assured there's plenty of danger. Besides weasels and raccoons, other mammals such as foxes, coyotes, and fishers enter the predatory picture. Grouse hens are masters of a trick that many mother birds employ when they feel a predator is too close to their young. The hen calls attention to herself with the most pitiable display of a feigned injury. She will drag her wing, make all sorts of commotion, and do her best to look like an easy supper. When the predator takes the bait and follows the faker, who skillfully manages to keep just beyond its reach, the children are left safely behind.

But the greatest threat—now and for the rest of their lives—comes from raptors, especially the great horned owl and the goshawk. Avoiding overhead predators is the reason that grouse prefer young forests with impenetrable brush and thick stands of saplings. By mid-July, with the chicks now larger than a dove, the dozen that hatched may now number five or six.

Those five or six have learned a lot traveling with mother and have grown remarkably good at filling their crops with the efficiency of the omnivore, supplementing insects with seeds and leaves, then berries, grapes, and apples. At four months, and full size, they get the message it's time to make their own way in the world. The males leave first and will travel a couple of miles in search of an available drumming log, which will become the center of its 6- to 10-acre domain for the rest of its life.

Within a couple of weeks, the females leave, dispersing even farther, and the territory they choose will likely overlap that of a cock from a different flock.

Of the original dozen, on average only three will survive the dispersal. But those that do will have developed skill in the evasive tactics that have earned the ruffed grouse such great respect. ∽

Sweetening the Melting Pot

Virginia Barlow

Most people, except perhaps those who are allergic to bee venom, believe that honeybees are about the best that the insect world has to offer. Humans have collected honey and beeswax since ancient times, and images of these industrious creatures were painted on the walls of a cave in Spain 8,000 years ago.

Charles Frederic Andros, a beekeeper and former New Hampshire bee inspector, harvests more than honey from his beehives. He uses pollen traps to brush pollen from bees as they return to the hive. He eats quite a bit of the pollen himself, sells some, and saves the rest to feed back to the bees in the spring. Before the willows and silver maples begin to flower in early spring, supplemental pollen encourages the queen to begin laying eggs.

The value of honeybees as pollinators has been recognized at least since the time of Aristotle, who is said to have been the first to see that a bee, whether in search of nectar or pollen, will visit only one kind of flower on a given foraging trip. If it were otherwise, they would make lousy pollinators. Because bees are faithful to one kind of flower on any given outing, it is estimated that almost a quarter of all the food eaten by humans is from species pollinated by bees.

Andros can tell many kinds of pollen apart by observing which plants are in flower, the color of the pollen, and its taste. He seems to know where each and every bee has been. And though they don't ignore native plants, it turns out that in Vermont and New Hampshire, honeybees make a good living from non-native plants, some of which are very much out of favor with the rest of us—the invasive exotics.

By mid-May, dandelions (originally native to Eurasia) provide the bees so much greenish yellow pollen that there is some to spare, and it's then that Andros places pollen traps at the entrances to the hives. By the end of May, apples (a popular introduced plant) are in full flower. A few days later, the non-native but well-named honeysuckles are producing nectar and a golden pollen. At about the same time, fields that are turned bright yellow by flowers of many mustard family members from Europe hum with bees.

Let's not forget that honeybees are not native to this hemisphere, either, but were brought by early sweet-toothed immigrants from Europe. Though some have escaped to the wild, more often they live in rectangular wooden structures and pay the rent with honey.

Honeybees originated in tropical Africa and moved north to colder climes before being domesticated. They differ markedly from almost all other temperate insects in being perennial. They don't overwinter in the egg, larval, or pupal stage like most other insects. Instead, the busy adults consume honey and use metabolic heat to keep their hives warm all winter long.

Bees love the tiny white flowers of glossy buckthorn, which blooms over a 3-month period beginning in June and produces honey that Andros says tastes like almond extract. Other honeybee favorites, such as sweet white clover, white Dutch clover, yellow clover, and bird's foot trefoil, are also imports, though their usefulness is usually thought to justify their presence. In early June, multiflora rose pollen is the dominant pollen in Andros's pollen trap trays. He says it's an orange-brown color, with a distinct rose flavor. In July I've often noted the bright orange pollen of asparagus (from Asia) on bees' legs as they come back to my hives. And bees love that most dreaded invasive species, purple loosestrife.

This bountiful harvest, from one flowering invasive plant after another, all summer long, reminds us of how much habitat has been disturbed by human activity and has therefore become susceptible to the incursion of opportunistic plants from other parts of the world. Often, once having gotten a foothold, these plants move into undisturbed meadows and marshes, displacing yet more native species in a pattern that is distressingly familiar to us. Sometimes the speed and magnitude of the invasion of these plants seems incredible; that they are consistently held in check in their native lands seems almost equally hard to believe.

Now, in late August, some beautiful native plants—a succession of different goldenrod species that grow abundantly in the fields and along roads in Vermont and New Hampshire—are helping our naturalized honeybees prepare for winter.

Trying to rid the countryside of all foreign plants is, at this point, unthinkable. Picking the right battles—worthwhile ones with a chance of succeeding—is our only option. And for me, appreciating that bad plants at least occasionally have a good side, and that some of these foreigners are now as beloved as the honeybee, helps a great deal. ∽

Sounds of the Season

∾

Madeline Bodin

I have a confession to make. Up until a week or so ago, I didn't know how to tell a grasshopper from a cricket. I'd see some sort of large, hopping insect, reach for my field guide, and—what is that thing?—could not come to a conclusion before it hopped away.

Now I know. It ain't easy. But more important, I had been approaching it all wrong. I was looking for grasshoppers to be in one group, with understandable grasshopper characteristics. And for crickets to be in another, with cricket characteristics. But it doesn't work that way.

There are indeed two groups, but they are both grasshoppers. One group is the short-horned grasshoppers, also known as locusts. The "horns" are antennae. In this group, the antennae are shorter than the length of the body, often less than half as long. Short-horns are generally active during the day, so if you see a grasshopper-like insect winging across your yard during daylight hours, it's most likely a short-horn.

The other group is the long-horned grasshoppers, which includes katydids and crickets. All of these have "horns" or antennae that are longer than their bodies. Crickets fold their wings flat down on their backs, while most of the other long-horned grasshoppers, including katydids, fold them tentlike above their backs. Members of the long-horned club move about and make most of their noise at night, so that insect chirping away under the supper table is apt to be a cricket (or other long-horned cousin).

Ross Bell, a professor emeritus at the University of Vermont, became interested in grasshoppers and crickets about 15 years ago. Not much was known about grasshoppers and crickets in Vermont then, and Bell feels that not all that much more is known about them now. "Grasshoppers don't sting people, so they don't get much attention," he says.

But Bell is keeping count. In Vermont, there are 39 species of short-horned grasshoppers, 16 species of crickets, and 17 other species of long-horned grasshoppers.

In New Hampshire, there are 35 short-horned grasshopper species, 15 crickets, 16 other species of long-horned grasshoppers, plus five camel crickets, a mole cricket, a pygmy mole cricket, and seven species of pygmy grasshoppers.

As for how the species tell themselves apart, it appears that sound is the main way. Bell says some people who collect crickets don't even collect their bodies, as most insect collectors do. They just record their songs.

"In some cases, you can't even tell the cricket species apart if you are holding them in your hand," Bell says, "but you can tell when they call."

Around my house at this time of year, the Carolina grasshopper is everywhere, erupting in short, noisy flights across the gravel driveway on its white-banded wings. This is a short-horned grasshopper, most active by day. It's found in both Vermont and New Hampshire. Bell notes that it is the most common grasshopper in both states. It can be quite colorful, he says: its wings are black with yellow borders, and a related species has wings that are sometimes yellow or pink.

Long-horned grasshoppers and crickets "sing" by rubbing a "scraper" on one wing against a "file" on the other wing. Some short-horned grasshoppers sing by rubbing a leg against a wing.

The "songs" of other short-horned grasshoppers are mechanical sounding—buzzes, whirrs, and clicks. The song of the house cricket goes *cheep-cheep-cheep* (pause) *cheep-cheep-cheep* (pause). The songs of other crickets, katydids, and the other long-horned grasshoppers can be complex, with chirps and buzzes and pauses. If you can hum along, then it's a cricket, advises one field guide. I'm not convinced that's entirely true, but it's a place to start.

Grasshoppers and crickets sing for pretty much the same reason birds do. The males sing to attract females and to stake out their territory. In some species, the females respond to the males with a song of their own.

Bell says it is not a myth: the temperature cricket, a kind of tree cricket, will tell you the temperature in Fahrenheit

if you count the number of chirps it makes in 15 seconds and then add 37. However, he adds, all grasshoppers and crickets sing faster when it is warmer and slower when it's colder. It's a function of their cold-blooded metabolism. When the weather is hotter, they do everything faster.

Personally, I'll use a thermometer when I need to know the temperature. But I'm keeping an ear out for the scritches, scratches, chirps, and hums of late summer and early fall. Now that I know that grasshoppers and crickets are easier to tell apart by sound than sight, I'll be listening more closely. ∽

Shrinking Streams Imperil Fish

Stephen Long

Take a look at any Connecticut River tributary in August, and you'll be hard-pressed to remember back to April when melting snow and spring rains filled it to its banks. At spring levels, it would have been a struggle to wade across; with each tentative step, you'd be fighting the heavy current. Today, you can surely find a spot where you can pick your way from rock to rock and cross to the other side without even getting your feet wet.

That seasonal change, so dramatic for visitors to the river, can be life threatening to the animals that live there: trout, smaller fish like dace and sculpins, and the macroinvertebrates they feed on.

Low water level means high water temperature. All trout require cold water, and of the three species in the Northeast, the brook trout (the only native) is most susceptible to warm water. More than a day or two at water temperatures above 77° Fahrenheit and brookies will go belly up. Rainbow trout and brown trout were imported to the region a century ago because they can handle slightly warmer temperatures, but the preferred temperature for all of them is within a few degrees of 60° Fahrenheit.

By August, temperatures in the slower, low-gradient tributaries are generally in the danger zone, which forces trout to congregate in stretches of nonlethal water. This was demonstrated to me one hot summer day wading the Waits River with three Vermont fisheries biologists conducting their annual census of trout populations.

In one 600-foot stretch of the river, despite it having the classic combination of riffles and pools that all fishermen associate with good trout habitat, there were only two spots that held trout. The first was where a tiny brook 12 inches wide met the river and pumped a steady stream of cold water into the head of a bend pool. Lined up tight to the bank like children at a drinking fountain was a pod of wild brookies, ten of them in all—not surprising since the water temperature elsewhere in this stretch was 73°.

In the next pool upstream, a similar number of brookies, along with a small brown and some hatchery rainbows, camped out in a three-foot-deep pool in the shade and shelter of a blown-down spruce. If it weren't for the cold brook and the mature spruce that had fallen into the river, there might not have been a single trout in this stretch of the Waits.

Living in pods like that is stressful for trout, which are naturally territorial. When the water cools at night, they reclaim their normal territory to feed.

Low water also forces the macroinvertebrates to move. As long as the drop in water level is gradual, many of them have the opportunity to crawl or swim to the safety of an underwater rock in the channel. While some—especially the burrowing insects—will be left high and dry to die, the rest will be concentrated in the section of river that is still wet. Stoneflies are particularly adept at moving when it becomes necessary. Even freshwater mussels—though at a snail's pace—are mobile.

Some rivers are worse than others in funneling all their life into a narrow summer channel. Those that run for miles alongside roads tend to ebb and flow dramatically. Rain falling on impervious road surfaces goes directly into the river, causing a surge in its level without adding a drop to the groundwater. Consequently, in periods when there is no rain, little groundwater is available to seep into the river.

Those rivers that are fed by springs and that flow through forestland are likely to maintain a more uniform flow and sustain much more life. Detritus (leaves, twigs, and other organic matter) is the building block of life for phytoplankton and zooplankton, which feed the macroinvertebrate community. When a river can stay bank full, and there are

eddies churning detritus, the river is like a rich stew. But when the river dries up to a narrow channel, the meat and vegetables are left to bake on the exposed cobbles and sandbars, and the river offers little more nourishment than stone soup.

That's why fisheries biologists are universal in their recommendation to maintain and enhance forested buffer strips along all rivers, streams, and brooks. Trees are an essential part of the river system: they provide a thick mat of roots to keep soil in place; they provide a steady supply of organic matter; they help recharge the groundwater; and they help keep the water clean and cold.

Forest cover helps, no matter how small the stream. The feeder brook that provided a life-giving shot of cold water to the trout in the Waits River did so because it flowed through continuous forest cover. ❧

Ambushed!

Ted Levin

I grew up watching Walt Disney's true-life adventures, where exotic animals from exotic lands paraded across a suburban movie screen for hour after uninterrupted hour. Music woven through Disney's footage set a mood, a pace, often at the expense of reality. Remember the dancing tarantulas in *The Living Desert*? A foot-stomping fiddle run overlaid what was probably a life-or-death struggle between two female spiders, converting them into merry, quixotic figurants, blithe beyond belief.

With this not quite in mind the other day, I found a honeybee apparently sipping nectar from a boneset flower that grows in the meadow in front of our house. The bee's long, tubular tongue extended like a New Year's party favor into one of the many quarter-inch white blossoms. Pollen dusted her legs. I stepped up to the flower and bent down so that my eyes were in line with the bee's. The bee, however, remained curiously still, as though suspended from the flower. I looked a little closer.

She was propped up from below the flower by the piercing and sucking mouthparts of two ambush bugs, one fixed to her throat, the other to her abdomen.

Yes, ambush bugs. Though not among the commonly known insects, ambush bugs are found in fields and meadows all across Vermont and New Hampshire from late summer through the first frost. They frequently attack and devour insects many times their own size, with their favorite meals including wasps, bees, flies, and butterflies.

An ambush bug selects a cluster of flowers, settles in, and waits for a potential meal to happen along. My particular boneset hosted light-colored ambush bugs—white and yellow with a hint of green, perfectly camouflaged. Later in August, yellow-brown bugs gather on goldenrod blossoms. Camouflage is a critical part of the ambush bug's feeding strategy, so finding these insects can be tricky. In general, the adults are between ¼- and ½-inch long, have short antennae, and appear somewhat triangular from above because they widen from front to back. From the side, ambush bugs look like miniature praying mantises.

Slow-moving predators, ambush bugs have modified forelegs that serve as powerful grasping organs. Their tibia—the distal end of the foreleg—is a small curved blade, like a miniature scythe, which snaps back into a groove on the short, thickened femur. Both tibia are armed with teeth. The entire leg looks like Popeye's arm: thin on either end, swollen in the middle.

When a bee lands near an ambush bug, the bug grabs it by any available body part: tongue, foot, antenna, or wing. Locked on, it probes the angry, thrashing bee, finds a soft spot, usually between the head and thorax or along the abdomen, and then inserts its hollow beak, pumping digestive enzymes that slowly make soup of the bee's innards. When the ambush bug is through feeding, all that is left of its victim is a dried husk.

As I watched the ambush bugs drain the honeybee, three parasitic flies, smaller than blackflies, settled on the bee's abdomen. They came for a free lunch. When the flies were done, they lumbered off, their transparent bellies swollen with predigested bee juice. Twenty minutes later, the ambush bugs, too, were sated. They disappeared back into the cluster of flowers.

The easiest way to find an ambush bug is to walk into a meadow at this time of year, look for flowering boneset, goldenrod, or milkweed, and examine the ground beneath the flowers for the dried husks of bees, wasps, or butterflies. Once you find these table scraps, carefully examine the underside of the flowers themselves for the well-concealed ambush bugs. Don't worry—though they could star in an insect horror movie, ambush bugs don't pose a danger to human hands.

I had approached some flowers in my meadow as many of us approach nature itself, expecting a benign and beautiful true-life adventure: *Pollination in a Wet Meadow*. Instead of a thirsty pollinator sipping nectar and inadvertently pollinating a flower, I found a hapless cadaver. The adventure was true to life, and beautiful in its own way, but the script was by Poe, not Disney. Like the bee, I had been ambushed by my own expectations. ∽

Mystery in the Forest

Madeline Bodin

Aimee Kidder hiked up a small rise and down into a dip in the forest floor. Then again, up and down across another dip. Aimee, an eighth-grader at Hartford Memorial Middle School in White River Junction, Vermont, and her classmates were searching the Hurricane Town Forest and Wildlife Refuge Park, not far from their school, for distinctive forest features as part of the Vermont Institute of Natural Science's Community Mapping program.

Ben Musson and two other students selected a slab of exposed roots from some tipped-over trees as their distinctive feature. Nearby, other kids chose a towering, seven-foot wall of roots from a toppled hemlock. Farther west, yet another group picked a grove of trees with oddly kinked trunks, which one young woman described as looking "like a cat's foot."

Clearly, some mystery was afoot. But while the thoughts of the young woman among the cat's-foot trees turned to something supernatural from *The Blair Witch Project*, the explanation for the weird landscape was more natural and closer at hand.

"A hurricane came through here," said Ben.

How did he know? The students were making connections between the name of the forest and an actual hurricane with the help of their teachers and Tom Wessels' book, *Reading the Forested Landscape*.

The book paints the scene of the devastating hurricane of September 21, 1938, which swept north up the Connecticut River valley before arcing west across Vermont. A quarter-million acres of forest were leveled. The storm left its mark of weird trees and walls of exposed roots on Hurricane Hill in Hartford, in the nearby town forest and refuge, and all across New Hampshire and Vermont.

Wessels explains that toppled trees often leave behind clues to explain what toppled them. Recognize the clues and you can figure out why the trees fell. A suspicious number of the trees in the Hurricane Town Forest were felled with their tops pointing toward the northwest—the distinctive calling card of the Hurricane of '38.

In your average forest, trees fall every which way. That's because a long-dead standing tree can be toppled by a strong wind from any direction, says Wessels. The clue that the tree was dead before it toppled is that decayed roots don't bring up much soil as they go over. A fallen dead tree tends to lie atop ground that is relatively undisturbed.

The chapter on the 1938 hurricane in Wessels' book is called "Pillows and Cradles." The title refers to the pit and mound landscape that develops in a forest after a large number of trees have been blown down while they were still living, such as after a hurricane. Unlike dead trees, live trees bring up a lot of earth with their roots when they go over. This divot of earth creates a "pit" or "cradle." Wessels calls it a cradle because the bare earth becomes a good place for small-seeded trees—such as birches, aspens, and pines—to sprout and grow. As the fallen tree rots, the earth in its roots drops into a pile, creating the corresponding "mound" or "pillow."

Strong blasts of air from summer thunderstorms also blow down live trees, not just dead ones. Since these storms usually arrive from the west, their winds leave tree trunks pointing from the northeast through the southeast. Find the average direction, says Wessels, and you'll see it is due east. Fallen trees with their tops pointing east is a strong sign, therefore, that they were blown down in a spring or summer thunderstorm.

Winter gales are also strong enough to knock over live trees. Wessels says that trees that fall toward the southeast and south usually have been felled by the arctic blasts of a fall or winter gale, whose strongest winds are usually out of the north and northwest.

Hurricane winds are complicated. They blow counterclockwise around the storm's eye, meaning that the direc-

tion a hurricane-blown tree falls depends on where it was in relation to the path of the storm. Wessels says trees that have fallen to the northwest are a clear sign of a hurricane, both because other storms won't fell a tree in that direction and because that was the direction of the blowdowns all across the Connecticut River valley from the 1938 hurricane.

As Aimee Kidder hiked up and down and up and down one day in the Hurricane Town Forest and Wildlife Refuge Park, something clicked. "Pillows and cradles," she thought, as she realized what she was walking over. Tree trunks pointing northwest. The Hurricane of '38. Mystery solved. ∽

September

FIRST WEEK

Blueberries are eaten by white-footed mice, chipmunks, skunks, and bears, as well as by many birds.

The ugliness of the nests of the fall webworm may be the worst thing about these gregarious caterpillars. The leaves they eat have done their job and would have been shed soon anyway.

Some yearling whitetail bucks leave their home territories, settling many miles from where they were born.

This year's turkey vultures have dark heads; the red, naked head comes with maturity.

Asters and goldenrods are the last food plants visited by honeybees.

SECOND WEEK

Purple-blue New England asters are blooming.

Crickets may move into buildings as they search for places to hibernate. Their incessant chirping can be aggravating at close range.

The usually solitary porcupine is on the prowl, looking for a mate.

Moose are mating.

The woods are quieter now, as fall bird migration is underway.

Snapping turtle eggs are hatching. Most hatchlings will head for water; some will overwinter where they hatch.

Black cherries are ripe and falling.

THIRD WEEK

3

Indian pipes, colorless, saprophytic plants of
deep shade, are turning their waxlike flowers
upwards, and the seeds are ripening.

Monarch butterflies are flying south, but
they seem to flap so lazily that you wonder
how they will ever get to Mexico.

Flickers are restless and gathered in flocks;
look for these plump, brightly colored
woodpeckers stalking ants on lawns.

New bumblebee queens will winter over in deserted
mouse burrows; the rest of the colony dies.

FOURTH WEEK

4

Crush a few leaves of sweet fern, a shrub of dry or
sandy soils, to recapture the fragrance of summer.

Crows are collecting and stashing
acorns. They can carry several at a time
in a pouch behind the lower bill.

Tree roots continue to grow. They'll grow
all winter, unless the ground freezes solid.

Woodchucks head for their winter quarters: deep,
grass-lined burrows that stay above freezing.

Mushrooms stuffed into tree crotches are
probably the work of the red squirrel.

Monarchs on the Move

Kent McFarland

The monarch flaps in my net as I reach in and carefully pull it out. My eight-year-old daughter peels an adhesive tag the size of my small fingernail from a sheet and gently sticks it on the middle of the butterfly's wing. This monarch will now be known as CAK 700, the code on its new wing tag.

Exactly what do we know about New England's monarch butterflies? For starters, they overwinter at just 13 known sites in the volcanic mountains of central Mexico. (A 1984 study found that there may have been as many as 60 overwintering sites, but commercial logging has eliminated most of them.) A single site may contain up to 4 million monarchs per acre and cover 0.1 to 8 acres of forest.

The butterflies arrive from the north between November and late December and generally hang out on the trees, metabolizing fat reserves that they have built up during migration. Remarkably, they actually gain weight on migration and arrive on the wintering grounds with fat reserves for the winter, unlike songbirds, which require huge fat stores to burn during migration.

The butterflies in the overwintering sites begin to disperse in March and early April, and they then migrate to the Gulf Coast of the southeastern U.S., where females arrive just as milkweed is sprouting. They lay eggs on the fresh plants and then die. One or two generations of monarch caterpillars feed on milkweed before it becomes too hot and dry for the milkweed to persist. The adult butterflies then continue the northward migration and arrive in New England at the end of May or early June, just as our milkweed is growing strong. The females lay eggs and die.

It takes about 30 days to go from a monarch egg to a monarch caterpillar. Beginning in mid-August, after several generations of monarchs have been born and died in New England, the decreasing daylight triggers a physiologic change in monarchs, causing them to migrate back to the wintering sites in Mexico and complete their yearly cycle. Incredibly, the adults that leave New England have never seen Mexico. Yet somehow they are guided back to these small sites.

The winter generation of butterflies lives up to eight months while the successive spring and summer generations are lucky to live a single month. It takes up to six generations of spring and summer monarchs to produce the final "super generation" that migrates to Mexico in the fall and then back to the southern United States in the spring.

How do we know that New England monarchs actually make it to Mexico and are not enjoying the winter in Florida or the Caribbean where there are some resident, non-migratory monarchs? Each fall, volunteers across New England capture monarchs and place tags on their wings. With over 10 million monarchs out there, the odds of a recapture are very poor. For example, in Vermont we have had only a few lucky folks. Despite my efforts, I am not one of them. There have been seven recaptures from (or from close to) Vermont, including one found in Mexico. The lucky tag was applied in Essex Junction on September 9, 1999, and the monarch was found in El Rosario, Mexico, on March 1st—2,320 miles away!

Hydrogen isotope analysis also shows that New England monarchs winter in Mexico. Rainwater contains slightly different amounts of these isotopes across North America, and this unique chemical signature is transferred from rainwater to milkweed to caterpillars to adult monarchs. By selecting 100 sites scattered across eastern North America, researchers have created a map displaying the chemical levels for each region.

I raised monarchs from laboratory stock on the Vermont Institute of Natural Science's Bragdon Preserve in Woodstock for this project in 1997 to contribute a Vermont site to the

project. Later in the year, researchers went to the 13 wintering sites in Mexico and gathered over 500 butterflies that had died of natural causes. They examined the levels of isotopes in these and found that 50 percent came from the midwestern corn and soybean belt and that a small percentage had indeed come from Vermont.

By September, the autumn monarch migration is in full swing. If you want to contribute more monarchs from your property for the flight south, consider cutting part of your milkweed patch by the end of July next year to produce succulent young milkweed shoots for the final generation. The females prefer to lay their eggs on these shoots rather than on fully grown milkweed that is in bloom.

My daughter checks to see if the tag has adhered to the monarch's wing. I note the date, location, and tag code in my notebook. The monarch flaps out of my grip, climbs high into the clear sky, and glides out of sight. Maybe CAK 700 will be our lucky tag. *Buen viaje, monarca!*

The Fountain of Youth

Chuck Wooster

Most people know that old-growth forest is rare in Vermont and New Hampshire—nearly every patch of forest hereabouts has felt the saw at least once since Colonial days. But what far fewer people know is that another type of forest is becoming increasingly rare around here: very young forest.

Early successional forest (the fancy term for very young forest) was our most common forest type in the twin states for much of the past two centuries. Settlers swarmed across our hills and valleys in the late 1700s and early 1800s, cutting down the forest to create farmland (especially sheep pasture), build buildings, lay in firewood, and even make a buck selling potash. Roughly three quarters of the forest was cut down. But by the middle of the nineteenth century, the wool market was collapsing and those upland soils were played out, leading farmers to abandon more than a million acres of pasture and hay fields.

What grew up to reclaim that land was early successional forest: raspberries, poplars, cherries, white pine, and a host of other forestland plants that need sunlight to sprout and that love the open conditions found in a very young forest.

Certain species of wildlife also love early successional forest, including two of our most beloved game animals: deer and grouse. These animals feed on the tender buds and branches of young trees and depend on the protection provided by the thick cover of young vegetation. Everyone who has walked in the woods has come across a patch of early successional forest, where sapling trunks are so close together that it can be hard to squeeze a human body in between them, let alone the body of a wolf or mountain lion in hot pursuit of a fawn. Deer and grouse can vanish into the interior of such thickets and know that they will have ample warning should a predator attempt to penetrate the maze.

Fifty to seventy-five years later, as the nineteenth century turned into the twentieth, much of the white pine forest that had grown up on the farms abandoned before the Civil War was logged off, and aggressive logging via river and railroad removed much of the old growth from the White Mountains and upper reaches of the Connecticut River valley. Early successional forest once again dominated the landscape of the twin states. Finally, after World War Two, when cheap transportation flooded New England with dairy products from farther west, river-bottom farms began to be sold off, setting off a third wave of early successional growth in our local forests.

Although Vermont and New Hampshire dairy farms continue to close, what grows in to replace them is often housing and other human development rather than brush and future forests. These aren't hill farms and marginal lands that are being abandoned but prime flat valley acres that make wonderful house lots. With most of our existing forests growing steadily older, therefore, and with very little new forest springing up from abandoned agricultural land, we face a situation that has been unknown for the last two centuries: early successional forest has become the exception rather than the rule.

Students of history will note that prior to Colonial settlement, early successional forest was also quite rare, meaning that we are now returning to a forest mix that is more similar to what we've had for the past thousand years than for the last few hundred years. But that is little consolation to those who love the fauna of the early successional forest, not just the deer and grouse but also the whippoorwill and woodcock, woodchuck and vole, beaver and broad-winged hawk. There's no danger of early successional forest taking over the joint these days, but increasing danger of it all but vanishing.

If you own a few acres and want to strike a blow for young for-est, consider opening a clearing here or there where sunlight can reach the forest floor and encourage new growth. Find a patch where the existing trees aren't headed for majesty, and either harvest the trees for firewood or simply drop them to the ground to create an opening. Or, if your holdings include more field than forest, consider letting the back forty revert to brush and raspberries. If you put the mower to a small portion of it every now and again, you'll have discovered the fountain of youth: a perpetual state of early succession.

Unlike old-growth forest, in which large tracts of land are required for an ecosystem to function effectively, young forests can make a contribution even if they're just pockets and postage stamps sprinkled here and there across the landscape. An acre or two of youth can make a world of difference in a forest that's otherwise becoming increasingly middle-aged. ∽

Wild Mice Split the Night Shift

Catherine Tudish

Just as we've always suspected, mice *do* work in shifts. How else could they get so much done? The two most common species of native mice in our region, deer mice and white-footed mice, are both nocturnal, but they prefer to work different hours. White-footed mice take the early shift and are generally active between 7 PM and 1 AM, while deer mice snooze past midnight and then get cracking from about 1 AM until 7 AM. What they do on their respective six-hour shifts is mostly find food and eat it; at this time of year, they are also hiding caches of food.

These two mice look very similar, and both, in fact, have white feet. Deer mice may look somewhat more deerlike, with their large ears, prominent black eyes, tawny brown coats, and white underparts. White-footed mice have more buff or gray in their coats and are slightly larger—they can grow to 7½ inches in length, compared to the deer mouse's average length of 6–7 inches. In both, the tail accounts for nearly half the body length. Mice of both species weigh approximately an ounce when fully grown. Ideally, they will consume about half an ounce of food every day, and they do not hibernate. In climates like ours, then, they must put by a large store of winter provisions.

Wild mice eat a variety of foods, including insects, spiders, moth and butterfly larvae, seeds, berries, acorns, fruits, and—when they can get it—cultivated grains such as corn and wheat. Deer mice and white-footed mice are good climbers and, like squirrels, often store nuts and seeds in tree cavities. Wild cherry pits and acorns are favorite foods to store, and, during the winter, the nibbled shells of both in a protected spot near the base of a tree are signs that a mouse nest is nearby.

At the same time mice are stocking up for the cold months ahead, they may be raising their last brood of the season. Females can have as many as four litters of young between April and October, with an average of four to six in each litter. They build nests in hollow logs, stone walls, wood piles, tree cavities, outbuildings, and even abandoned birds' nests. Unlike the average bird nest, a mouse nest is covered on the top with an entrance on the side, so a mouse moving into a bird nest must do some remodeling. Mice line their nests with soft plant material such as shredded bark and moss and are always on the lookout for other cushy fibers such as thread or bits of fur.

Newborn mice are altricial—that is to say naked, blind, and helpless. Their eyes and ears are closed at birth, and their skin is so transparent that milk is visible in their stomachs after they nurse. They grow quickly, though, and are weaned by the age of 3 weeks. After mating, adult mice live separately, but male deer mice do return to the nest to help groom the young and teach them how to find food.

Though mice are prolific breeders, they are also the prey of several larger nocturnal animals, and thus their numbers are kept in check. For many owl species, mice are the mainstay of the diet. Mice are also preyed upon by weasels, snakes, skunks, raccoons, and other animals. For this reason, mice tend to eat in protected places, such as under a rock overhang or among exposed tree roots.

Despite Robert Burns's characterization of them as "cow'ring, timorous beasties," deer mice and white-footed mice have the right stuff. Not only are they agile climbers but strong swimmers, too. And they have a remarkable homing instinct. In a series of experiments at the University of Michigan, white-footed mice captured and then released two miles away routinely found their way back to the very spot where they were captured.

Skeptics aside, rarely do these mice come into our houses in the fall—those are the gray European house mice invading our pantries and building nests between the walls. If you want to spend time in the company of native mice, you need to go outside at night, preferably into a wooded area. You may hear faint scratchings on the trunks of trees or rustlings in the fallen leaves, or possibly the drumming sound mice make by tapping a dry stalk or leaf with their front feet. If you want to know whether you're hearing a white-footed mouse or a deer mouse, check your watch. ∾

Scientists Reverse Acid Rain

Geoff Wilson

We in northern New England continue to contend with acid rain. A report released by the Environmental Protection Agency in 2003 stated that, despite a decrease in the acidity of incoming rain, much of New England has not seen a corresponding improvement in its surface waters because decades of acid rain have removed many of the soil elements that naturally neutralize acidity. Since these elements, primarily calcium but also magnesium and potassium, are also important for tree growth, ecosystem scientists in the Northeast have become very interested in what is happening to our forests when these important nutrients are removed.

Soils in our region tend to be naturally acidic to begin with, which makes them especially vulnerable to the additional acidity from acid rain. When acid rain moves through the soil, positively charged hydrogen ions in the rainwater (acidity is a measure of hydrogen ions) switch places with positively charged ions—mostly calcium—that are loosely held in the soil. The water draining from the soil is thus less acidic than the rainfall, since it lost hydrogen ions to the soil, but the soil is left with a reduced ability to continue this process in the future since it has lost calcium.

Calcium is a vital nutrient for tree health, and calcium deficiency has been tied to sugar maple decline and winter injury in red spruce. It's also important in other ways: birds need calcium for eggshells; plants need it for a variety of things, including cell walls; and soil pH, largely controlled by calcium, influences the availability of other nutrients to plants.

Clearly, acid rain has the potential to significantly affect our forests, but in what ways? An ambitious, 50-year experiment at the Hubbard Brook Experimental Forest (HBEF), in Woodstock, New Hampshire, aims to answer this question.

The HBEF is a 7,800-acre study area within the White Mountain National Forest with 10 small, forested watersheds in which the cycling of water and nutrients has been measured intensively for the past 40 years. This makes the HBEF a perfect study site for two reasons. First, there is a precise record of the chemical constituents of the rain and streamwater for much of the acid rain era. This record, in fact, led to the discovery of acid rain in the late 1960s and now has enabled scientists to measure just how much calcium has been lost from the forest since the study began. Second, the presence of a group of similar watersheds within the HBEF enables scientists to manipulate one whole watershed and compare its behavior with a second "control" watershed nearby.

This is just what the scientists at the HBEF have been doing—they've replaced the amount of calcium lost to acid rain in an entire 29-acre watershed and are now analyzing what happens to all of the components of the treated watershed (plants, animals, microbes, fungi, soils, and streams) compared with an adjacent, untreated watershed. By watching how the calcium gets incorporated into the forest and how the forest then begins to differ from that in the untreated watershed, scientists hope to quantify the role calcium plays in both the structure (what and how much is there) and function (how elements flow through) of northeastern forests.

In the fall of 1999, the calcium study at Hubbard Brook began when 45 tons of a calcium-rich mineral called wollastonite were spread by helicopter evenly over the 29-acre watershed. This amount was calculated to equal the calcium lost to acid rain. The calcium was expected to take seven years to be fully absorbed into the environment, and the study itself is envisioned to last 50 years, so very few results are yet available. Some preliminary observations, however, are worth noting.

Levels of available calcium in the organic layer of the soil are significantly higher than they were before the application. Calcium levels in some plants, like wood fern, shot up the year after application. Higher levels of calcium are also showing up in some tree species

even though the trees did not respond immediately. In 2003, sugar maple seedlings were measurably greener in the calcium-treated watershed. Perhaps most tantalizing was the observation that, in the higher elevations, where red spruce grows, the spruce appeared to experience less winter injury than in the nearby control watershed.

It will be years before scientists have a good grasp on how the forest responds to the removal of this acid rain stress, but the process should lead to a better understanding of the relationship between soils and the properties of the forests they support. The old saying about planting apple trees applies equally well to long-term scientific studies: the best time to get started was 50 years ago. But the second-best time is now. ⁂

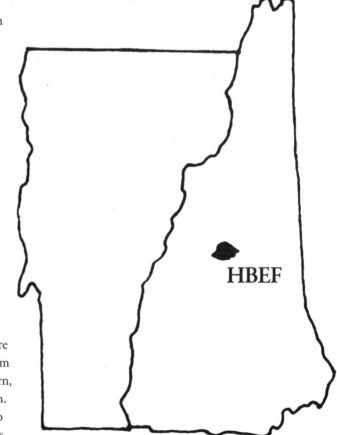

HBEF

A Good Year for Fir Cones

Kent McFarland

I am hanging from the top of a 25-foot balsam fir tree, 3,500 feet up a mountain on a breezy day, counting cones. For more than a decade, I have been studying the fir forests high in the Green Mountains with other biologists from the Vermont Institute of Natural Science.

Since 1920, when a biologist in New Brunswick began monitoring balsam fir cone production, it has been known that balsam firs produce heavy cone crops in odd years and few or no cones in even years. Between 1920 and 1950, this two-year cycle only broke three times. More recently, forest ecologists recorded the same cycle in the Adirondacks and the Green Mountains. On top of that, it appears that balsam fir productivity is synchronized across the Northeast—for three years, I drove from Vermont to Newfoundland and found all the trees to be in perfect synchrony each time.

But this is only the beginning of the story. The cone cycle also ties together red squirrels and birds.

Cones form on the trees in the spring, and by August, if there's going to be a big crop, you can see the cones standing on the ends of tree branches like green candles. After just a few years of data collection, we could predict next summer's squirrel and bird populations by looking at the fall cone crop—lots of cones one year meant lots of crossbills, pine siskins, and red squirrels the next. But it also meant that most other songbirds' nesting success was going to be terrible.

Crossbills, siskins, and red squirrels dine on the seeds hidden away inside the cones. Crossbills and siskins are so specialized and dependent on these crops that we rarely see a single individual in the summer following a bad cone crop. I have often wondered how crossbills know to immigrate into the region when there are many cones and to stay away when there are none; it turns out that the cone crops are regular enough that crossbills can be certain of food if they arrive only every other year.

What about red squirrels? Most research suggests that squirrels live longer than two years, so how do they make it? Perhaps they migrate up and down the sides of the mountains, between hardwood and coniferous forests. When cone crops are big, the squirrels move up the mountains to the conifers, and when crops fail, they move back down.

In mid-May, when we arrive at one of our research sites atop Mt. Mansfield, the crossbills and siskins have already finished breeding, and there are juveniles flying about in large flocks. Breeding may begin as early as January. If cones are especially plentiful, the crossbills and siskins may raise several families before the seeds become scarce. But by the end of May, the cones are stripped, and the remaining seeds are lying on the melting snow.

Red squirrel populations (and probably those of other small mammals) rise dramatically following good cone years, and that spells disaster for summer-nesting songbirds like Bicknell's thrush and blackpoll warblers. The squirrels have a peak mating period from January to February. Females are then pregnant for about 40 days, and the young spend another 30 days in the nest before venturing out onto the family's territory, just about the time the songbirds are laying eggs.

Red squirrels and other small mammals have a taste for eggs and nestlings. Each year, we spend hundreds of hours finding and monitoring songbird nests in these forests, and we've found a clear two-year cycle closely following previous fall cone production and the accompanying high squirrel populations. Every other summer is a bad year for most nesting songbirds in the mountaintop forest because the red squirrels have dined on eggs and nestlings.

But crossbills and siskins also breed in high cone years, when red squirrel populations are elevated, so how do they deal with the squirrels? Why aren't their nests plundered, too? These birds have several advantages. They nest in late winter when there are lots of cones for the mammals to eat and the young squirrels have not yet ventured out of the nest. Crossbills and siskins tend to pick taller and more isolated trees for nesting, with fewer cones on them, so squirrels are less likely to stumble upon them. And they often nest semicolonially in trees, which gives them more eyes to watch out for red squirrels and attack them if they come near.

It doesn't end there. We have a sneaking suspicion that the saw-whet owls that feed on the voles and mice that feed on the seeds may also be tied into the cone cycle. The deeper we dig, the farther the cone cycle seems to reach. ∾

Northern Lights Going Out?

Chuck Wooster

We humans have a knack for believing that everything was better, more vivid, more extreme, or at least more memorable when we were younger. The snow was deeper. The foliage was more beautiful. The summers were cooler. Or warmer. Either way, better.

Usually the facts don't bear this out. But sometimes they do.

Take the northern lights. I remember standing in downtown Hanover, New Hampshire, after supper in the winter of 1989 and watching bright red northern lights cover more than half the sky—plainly visible through the glare of the streetlights. The following summer, northern lights were so common over Vermont and New Hampshire that, on almost any clear night in July and August, you simply had to walk outside after dark to see a light show straight out of an Arctic photo-shoot in *National Geographic*.

I confess I started taking the northern lights for granted. But not anymore, now that they're gone.

Well, they aren't exactly gone, but they are less common than they used to be. The reason has to do with changes in the amount of energy being put out by the sun, or more prosaically, the sunspot cycle.

When dark spots appear on the surface of the sun (seen only through special telescopes, that is—don't try this at home!), they usually precede an eruption of energy from the sun's surface called a solar flare. These flares release bursts of energy that travel across the emptiness of space, reaching the earth two to four days later and flooding the top of the atmosphere with charged particles called ions. Sometimes these bursts of ions are so intense that they interfere with telecommunications satellites and radio signals from the ground.

These energy storms also create the northern lights. As the ions enter the earth's magnetic field, they become concentrated at the north and south magnetic poles, much like iron filings attracted to the poles of a magnet. Over the poles, the ions energize the oxygen and nitrogen atoms that are found at the top of the atmosphere, causing them to glow. If this sounds rather far-fetched, it's essentially the same way that your television set works: a stream of ions from the back of the set hits the screen, causing the elements behind the screen to glow and emit light. (This is an "old-fashioned" TV we're talking about, not the newfangled flat-screen job you've been pondering.)

Greenish gray is the most common color for the northern lights, but red appears in more intense episodes, along with various shades in between. Over the north magnetic pole, the phenomenon is called the aurora borealis. Over the south, it's the aurora australis. Because the two poles of a magnet can never be isolated from one another (you can never have a north pole existing all by itself, without a complementary south pole somewhere nearby), whenever the northern lights are taking place, the southern lights are in full swing at exactly the same moment.

Although ions are constantly bathing the earth, the more sunspots occur, the more common it is to see the northern lights because they will be brighter and visible much farther south from the pole. Nearly a thousand years of observations by astronomers has shown that sunspot activity follows an 11-year cycle. At the peak of the cycle, there are 10 times more sunspots occurring than there are at the bottom of the cycle.

You guessed it: 1989/1990 was the peak of a sunspot cycle. Right now, in 2005, we're at the bottom. There's still a chance of seeing northern lights these days, but the displays are fewer (meaning you'll have to stay up a lot of nights hoping to see them) and fainter (meaning you'll have to stay up very late to catch the sky at its darkest).

The mathematically inclined among you will have noticed that I just skipped from 1990 to 2005, meaning that there must also have

been a sunspot peak in 2001, which there was. It just wasn't as intense as the 1990 peak and didn't lead to night after night of marvelous light shows over Vermont and New Hampshire.

Astronomers have also noticed that the sunspot peaks themselves follow a cycle, and that the 1990 peak was the third largest in more than 300 years. Though it's impossible to forecast the sun's future activity with great precision, astronomers believe that upcoming sunspot peaks will not be as bright as the 1990 peak for a long time to come. So mark your calendar for the 2012 display. The northern lights may not be as bright as they were back in the last century, but at the very least you'll have a great opportunity to say, "back when I was a kid…" ∾

October

⁓

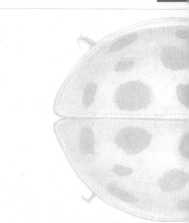

OCTOBER

FIRST WEEK

Dry days will cause milkweed pods to open, releasing
streams of fluffy parachutes and seeds.

The beautifully colored leaves of white ash, in
all shades of purple, are among the first to fall.

Only the hardiest of the migrating
songbirds are still here: bluebirds,
phoebes, robins, white-throated sparrows,
and the occasional hermit thrush.

Wood turtles return to streams,
spending the winter submerged
beneath a bed of muck and leaves.

Geese, geese, and more geese.

SECOND WEEK

Bears are especially active in the fall, eating
everything they can find to store enough
fat to last for the next five months.

Look for the long, toothed, evergreen
leaves of pipsissewa, a handsome,
small plant of dry woods.

Beavers may be working long hours, not
just in the nighttime, accumulating enough
branches to feed themselves through the winter.

White-throated sparrows are singing
their spring song, but at this time of
year, they rarely get it quite right.

THIRD WEEK

3

Sparrows moving through may include chipping, fox, song, white-throated, white-crowned, and Lincoln.

Witch hazel is in flower, the last woody plant to flower in the Northeast.

Large flocks of snow geese may be taking a several-day rest stop in wetlands.

Ruffed grouse are growing their "snowshoes"— seasonal horny extensions to their toes that will allow them to walk on top of the snow.

Last woodcocks head south, as the ground freezes and worms become unavailable.

FOURTH WEEK

4

Fishers are eating apples, berries, and nuts. Their diet does not consist entirely of small mammals and house cats.

Chipmunk cheek pouches are bulging with sugar maple seeds.

Apple trees may not have colorful leaves, but they certainly have colorful fruits; look for mammals and birds harvesting the bright red and yellow apples.

Catbirds are fattening up on almost any fruit or berry you can think of. They will soon leave to winter from the Gulf Coast south to Costa Rica.

Seeing Spots

Madeline Bodin

Who loves a ladybug? Until recently, everyone did. These tiny beetles gobble aphids and other soft-bodied insects that plague crops and ornamental plants.

It is said that their name refers to the Virgin Mary, to whom our European ancestors gave thanks for the beetles that saved their crops. They are also called lady beetles. In Britain, they are called ladybirds or ladybird beetles. For centuries, they were thought of as bringers of good luck. In Iran, they are called "Good News."

As far as we know, the name has nothing to do with feminine characteristics. There are, indeed, gentleman ladybugs. Ladybugs share a basic body plan with their fellow beetles, which includes the wings that let them "fly away home." It's the hard forewings that give a ladybug its shell-like covering. The large, membranous hindwings underneath unfold and are used for flying.

The high-water mark for ladybug love may very well have been in 1977, when the New Hampshire legislature named the two-spotted ladybug as that state's official insect. (Massachusetts, Ohio, and Tennessee had already made ladybugs their state insects.) In 1989, New York designated the widespread and common nine-spotted ladybug as its state insect.

There are some 450 native species of ladybug in North America and several thousand species in the world. New Hampshire has about 60 native species within its borders, and Vermont has about 40. Almost every one of those species is a beneficial insect, eating plant pests that we might otherwise use chemicals to kill.

But sometime in the 1990s, the worm, or maybe in this case the larva, began to turn. (Ladybug larvae are spiky-looking things, often equal in size to mom and dad.) Ladybugs have always overwintered as adults in large groups, sometimes even in people's houses. As the 1990s went on, more and more people in the eastern, midwestern, and northwestern U.S. were complaining about hundreds or thousands of ladybugs entering their homes in the fall.

While the two-spotted, native ladybug had always done this to some extent, the new culprit was the multicolored Asian lady beetle (*Harmonia axyridis*), also known as the Halloween ladybug. This ladybug is a tree-dweller, originally from Asia, and it comes in a variety of shades, from yellow to orange to red.

This ladybug had been intentionally re-leased time and again—in Georgia, Ohio, and Washington—throughout the 1970s as a natural predator of crop pests. When few of these ladybugs were recaptured, it was thought they were dying out. Instead, they had just flown away to new homes. The good news is that these ladybugs did such a number on the pecan aphids in Georgia that chemical pesticides are no longer used for aphids there. The bad news is that every fall, Halloween la-dybugs find their way into American homes, sometimes in horror-movie-like numbers.

Ladybugs don't eat while inside your house, and they don't reproduce there. They are just seeking a warm place for the winter, which may be a small solace when you find one do-ing the backstroke in your coffee.

The bugs can be kept out by tightly sealing your house, including putting screens over all roof, attic, and wall vents. If they are already inside, ladybugs can be sucked up with a vacu-um cleaner that has a nylon stocking inserted into the extension wand. The ladybugs that get in your house are usually non-native and, quite obviously, overabundant, so do with them what you will.

Just don't crush them. They stain. And don't eat them.

"They taste horrible, which is part of their natural defense and why many of them are brightly col-ored—an example of aposomatic (warning) coloration," says John Weaver, who, as an entomologist with the New Hampshire De-partment of Agriculture, I trust did not arrive at this knowledge through his own experience.

He says that winemakers have found that when Halloween ladybugs get harvest-ed with the grapes, the crushed beetles taste so bad they can ruin the wine.

We won't be rid of the Halloween ladybug any time soon, but we may have learned our lesson. Weaver reports that "the U.S. Depart-ment of Agriculture seems to have adopted new guidelines in selecting lady beetles for in-troduction, selecting species that are special-ized predators and not selecting species that are generalized predators."

Introduced ladybug species don't just bug humans. They affect other ladybugs as well. New York hasn't seen its state insect—the nine-spotted—in years. It's believed that a dif-ferent introduced species, the seven-spotted ladybug, may have done it in either by eating it or by outcompeting it.

It's a little harder to love a ladybug these days, but it's a little harder to be one, too. ⌒

Fog, Foliage, and Frost

Chuck Wooster

Our organic vegetable farm sits deep in the Connecticut River valley, a few hundred feet above the river and more than a thousand feet below the top of the valley's walls. On autumn mornings, we are often submerged in a sea of fog; the tide doesn't recede some days until as late as noon.

We plan our final harvest week of the season to coincide with peak foliage, which is roughly the middle of October where we live. This is not to attract leaf peepers to our farm, which sits at the end of a dirt road, far from the main tourist routes. Rather, it is for the simple reason that foliage prevents frost.

Well, "prevents" may be too strong a word, but it is certainly safe to say that foliage "mitigates" or "reduces the impact of" frost in the deep crevices of the river valleys of New Hampshire and Vermont.

The key link between foliage and frost is fog. Most people believe that the reason we have so much fog in the fall is because the night sky is growing ever colder, causing moisture in the air to condense into fog. This is true. Especially on clear, still nights, when heat from the ground radiates up into the sky, fog banks can grow to hundreds of feet thick

by morning. The cold night sky of autumn explains why fog is a fall phenomenon: the night sky of summer is rarely cold enough to turn all that humidity into fog.

But the cold of autumn is only half the story. In November, for example, the sky is even colder than it is in October, yet fog is not very common. Why not? Because there isn't enough moisture in the air. That's where the foliage comes into play.

Trees are enormous consumers of water, and nearly all of the water they consume is released through the leaves into the air as part of photosynthesis. Indeed, just over half of all the rain that falls on our forests during the year is taken up by trees and respired into the air. Some very rough back-of-the-envelope calculations: 36 inches of rain falling on the 5 million acres of the Connecticut River valley in a year translates into 15 million acre-feet of water. At 325,000 gallons per acre-foot and 225 days of foliage growth per year, that's roughly 7 billion gallons of water that our forests release into the air over the Connecticut River on a typical day. Give or take a billion. When the leaves are on the trees.

Once the leaves have fallen, however, this moisture conveyor belt is turned off. Trees are dormant. The 7 billion gallons go away. Fog becomes rare.

Another way to recognize this phenomenon is to observe the amount of water flowing in our brooks and streams in the fall. Once the trees lose their leaves, stream flows rise as all those gallons that would have been taken up by the trees find their way into the brooks instead. The ground in November is often soggy underfoot where it was dry in September, even with equivalent amounts of rainfall.

Back on the farm, autumn fog helps protect our crops in three ways. First, thick fog acts like a blanket on clear nights, trapping heat near the ground and shielding tender crops from direct exposure to the night sky. Second, water vapor releases heat into the air as it condenses into fog, and while that heat isn't enough to overcome a major drop in temperature, it can be enough to keep an overnight low temperature just above freezing rather than just below—a crucial difference to the vegetable grower. Finally, fog helps

insure that the crops have plenty of moisture; a well-hydrated plant is better able to avoid frost damage than a desiccated plant.

Once the leaves are down and the fog dries up, our location deep in the river valley works against the growing of crops. Overnight temperatures drop significantly as the cold night air sliding off the hills pools deep in the valley. Our farm, which was warmer than those on the high hilltops during the early autumn, suddenly becomes much colder once the fog is gone. No foliage means no fog; no fog means more frost.

In 2005, my final vegetable harvest didn't coincide with peak foliage. September was exceptionally warm and reasonably wet. By early October, the foliage had barely begun to turn. We had to call it a season anyway, given that we hadn't planted enough crops to harvest deep into October. But it sure was odd to be gathering in the leeks and Brussels sprouts under blue skies and green leaves, with not a hint of impending frost. ∽

The Problem of Porcupines

∾

Catherine Tudish

By ordinary human standards, porcupines have many bad habits. Besides extricating their quills from the noses of pet dogs and livestock, humans must throw out axe handles and leather harnesses chewed beyond use. Porcupines damage, and sometimes kill, trees by gnawing on them; they even gnaw at uninhabited wooden buildings. The human response to porcupines is often an attempt to eradicate them by shooting, trapping, or poisoning.

This wasn't always so. Among Native Americans in northern New England and elsewhere, the porcupine was prized for its quills, which were dyed and used in decorative work. In winter, especially, porcupines were an important source of meat—honored, along with animals such as deer, for their life-giving qualities. Though porcupines were common in the forests, their numbers were held in check by their main predator, the fisher.

Eventually, Native Americans began to hunt fishers for their fur. Then European colonists further depleted fisher populations by trapping them and deforesting the southern part of their range. With a scarcity of natural predators, porcupines have flourished throughout New Hampshire, Vermont, Maine, and eastern Canada.

Given the porcupine's unique defense system, it's easy to see why most predators leave them alone. As naturalist Paul Rezendes notes, the porcupine's scientific name—*Erethizon dorsatum*—translates as "the animal with the irritating back." While they appear prickly at all times, porcupines actually have a soft brown undercoat and coarser, longer guard hairs tipped with white that cover the quills. Fully grown, a porcupine weighs between 10 and 15 pounds and has 30,000 of these hollow, tapering, barb-tipped quills. Longest on the back and tail, the quills are raised when the porcupine senses danger, pushing the guard hairs forward to form an intimidating crest.

Approached by humans or other threatening animals, porcupines prefer to scurry away and climb a tree. Failing this, a porcupine will try hiding its face and belly—which have no quills—and presenting its back. As a last resort, it will release as many as several hundred quills by slapping an invader with its quill-studded tail. Embedded in flesh, the barbs will swell, driving the quills in deeper and making them difficult and extremely painful to remove.

No one seems surprised to learn that porcupines are mostly solitary animals. Nearsighted, slow-moving, they make their dens in rock ledges or hollow trees close to a good food supply. In our region, hemlock is a favorite food source and the mainstay of the porcupine's winter diet. Although they don't hibernate, porcupines curtail their activity and their range during the winter, never venturing far from their dens. Porcupine dens are easiest to spot in winter, when there will be large accumulations of scat around the entrances and hemlocks with partially stripped branches nearby.

The sedentary winter is the gestation period for the single porcupine offspring that will be born in April or May, its parents having enjoyed an extremely brief, if sweet, courtship in late October or early November. At the age of one or two, the female will go into heat for 8-12 hours, attracting the attention of males who follow her around, grunting and humming. Once she chooses her partner, the female engages in a kind of dance with him. Standing on their hind feet, the male and female embrace, placing their paws on each other's shoulders and rubbing noses, whining and grunting all the while. They may cuff one another playfully before eventually falling to the ground, when the female obligingly flattens her quills and moves her tail out of the way. Once they have mated, the porcupines go their separate ways—despite their previous displays of affection.

Winter might be considered their "social season," for porcupines are likely to group together in the choicest winter denning areas. Although they ignore each other, except for teeth-chattering over disputed food, as many as 100 porcupines have been found in large rock piles, and six were discovered living together in an abandoned house in New Hampshire.

Believed to chew wood and leather for the salt left in it from perspiration, porcupines also need to hone their continuously growing teeth, which may explain why they gnaw at buildings. While tools can easily be stored out of a rodent's reach, what about the damage porcupines do because of their appetite for the bark and buds of sugar maple, birch, white pine, hemlock, and fruit trees?

People can protect their orchards and plantations with electric fencing or by installing a 30-inch band of sheet metal or aluminum flashing around the base of individual trees. Liquid repellents available at hardware stores can also be brushed or sprayed on trees and buildings. If this seems like too much trouble, maybe it's time for a change of attitude. As a biologist once told me when I complained about cluster flies, "You just have to appreciate biodiversity." ∾

Fall Foliage and Climate Change

Michael J. Caduto

Forest scientists who study global warming in the Northeast say that a warmer climate could lead to later and lackluster leaf peeping. Three different things could cause this to happen, acting alone or in combination.

Records kept by the National Oceanographic and Atmospheric Administration reveal that the average annual temperature in the region that includes New England and New York has increased by 0.7° Fahrenheit during the past 100 years. Computer models project that the average annual temperature will rise much faster, from between 6° and 10° Fahrenheit over the next 100 years.

Barry Rock, a professor of natural resources at the University of New Hampshire, predicts that, based on two climate models in a regional climate assessment study, "Within the next 100 years, Boston could have a climate similar to either Richmond, Virginia, or Atlanta, Georgia." At this rate, says Rock, "In 100 years, New England's cooler regions will no longer promote the growth of sugar maples, which are well adapted to the region's current climate."

That's the first way that global warming could affect leaf peeping—the loss altogether of the sugar maple, whose wide range of yellow, orange, and red leaves makes New England's foliage so impressive.

David Kittredge, a professor of natural resource conservation at the University of Massachusetts and forest policy analyst at the Harvard Forest, sees several scenarios. "If we get a climate more like that of Pennsylvania, Maryland, or West Virginia, we could still have a sugar maple component in our forests." Of five computer models created by the U.S. Forest Service to predict the geographic shift in the ranges of forest species, only one foretells that global warming will cause sugar maples to disappear from parts of New England.

Global warming may also directly affect the hues of autumn leaves. In part, the colors of fall foliage result from the breakdown of chlorophyll, the green pigments in leaves that normally mask the background yellow, orange, and brown pigments. Reds and purples, however, are actually created in the leaves each autumn.

Abby van den Berg, a research technician at the University of Vermont's Proctor Maple Research Center, says that fall leaf colors are initiated by shortening day length and decreasing temperature. "If you change the timing of the onset of cool temperatures, you alter when chlorophyll breakdown starts. Even though we have no good way to predict how climate change will affect the process that creates the colors of foliage season, it will change how the landscape will look over time."

The first hard frosts, which bring out the most vibrant leaf colors, used to occur around the third week in September. But in recent years, these frosts have arrived later. In 2004, the first hard frost in many parts of the North Country didn't come until mid-October. Although Columbus Day has traditionally marked the height of foliage season in northern New England, the timing of peak fall leaf color is shifting toward mid- to late October.

Predicting the timing and intensity of fall foliage colors seems to be as much art as it is science. When trees are stressed, perhaps due to a summer drought or even too much rain, they tend to develop particularly bright red fall leaf colors, regardless of a changing climate. Dr. Tim Perkins, director of the Proctor Maple Research Center, says, "It is premature to ascribe recent muted foliage to global warming. Here in Underhill Center, Vermont, we had a spectacular and long foliage season in 2004."

Barry Rock predicts that foliage season will gradually come later and the intensity of colors will decrease. Using Earth-orbiting satellite data collected by NASA and the National Oceanographic and Atmospheric Administration from the 1970s to the present, Rock is analyzing the autumn dates of the onset of red hues in the northern forests. This research will paint a picture of how, and whether, the timing and intensity of the foliage season is shifting.

The third possible link between global warming and a reduced foliage display comes from the ongoing threat to the region's sugar maples from something that forest scientists are calling "maple decline." Says Rock: "Hot summer months are likely to be poor air-quality months characterized by acid rain events. Ground-level ozone is another pollutant that may predispose trees to being weakened or killed. Sugar maple, red spruce, and white pine are all struggling. Acid rain and global climate change are two faces of the same beast."

If global warming does lead to a decline in the beauty of our autumn foliage, the negative economic impact on New England would be substantial. But more than that, it would be a tragedy. Fall foliage is woven into the fabric of New England's identity, and it is an iconic event by which we celebrate the seasons. ∽

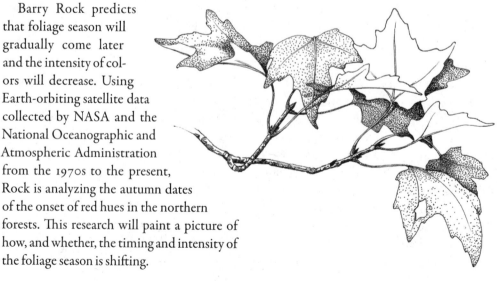

What You See Isn't What You'll Get

Chuck Wooster

We've all fallen for it at some point, those of us who spend time in the woods: the way it looks now is the way it always has looked. And the way it always will look.

And why not? When you're deep in a grove of towering pines or enjoying the sunlight filtering through a glade of birches, it's tempting to believe that the trees have always been there, providing solace or refuge or beauty right down through the ages. But it's not true.

In fact, if someone (such as a nephew or grandchild) were to ask you to predict what trees would be growing in the woods 100 years from now, your safest bet would be to say, "Not what's here now." That's the general rule: what you see is not what you'll get.

Take white birch, for example, a tree that can grow in almost-pure stands. Although it's hard to imagine whole groves going by the board, they almost certainly will. White birch is a relatively short-lived species (averaging less than a hundred years) that requires sunlight for seed germination. The sum of these two factors is certain obsolescence: when the adults topple over, the trees waiting to emerge from the shadows won't be birches.

The case of red oak and white pine is particularly unusual. One tends to replace the other. Or, said another way, a great place to find a young oak forest growing is underneath a mature grove of pines, and vice versa. Although this seems counterintuitive from the "germinates in sunlight" perspective, it's not. White pine germinates in sunlight, while red oak can germinate almost anywhere, but more often in shade. In the oak/pine case, there is another factor at play: squirrels and chipmunks. Both tree species are used by the rodents for food and cover, and given the animals' propensity to scatter and bury seeds for later consumption, and their tendency to commute back and forth between pines and oaks, they may be the dominant force in changing the forest from one tree species to another. Sort of a Johnny Appleseed effect.

Actually, apple trees are another good example. If you find an old apple tree in the woods, you almost certainly won't find an apple tree there a few hundred years hence. The apple is not native to Vermont and New Hampshire, so its presence in the woods means that it was planted at some point in the past, either by homesteading humans or by opportunistic animals (who raided the homesteaders' trees.) But deer love to eat new apple seedlings and our taller native trees are able to overtop the adults, so apple trees usually do not beget apple trees.

Hemlock is another example of animal intervention. Thick stands can last for centuries, and sometimes do, but deer love to spend the winter under the protection of the boughs, nibbling all the while on young hemlock seedlings. Sooner or later, the original hemlocks die of old age or natural calamity. But with no new hemlocks waiting to fill the gap, other pioneer species move in. When deer populations are high, the animals inadvertently damage the hemlock groves they depend on.

Although "what you see isn't what you'll get" is the general rule, there are, of course, exceptions. On certain sandy and acidic soils, white pine will be able to hold off all competitors for generations, leading to those scattered spots around the region with groves named "the cathedral pines" or some such. The hemlock groves mentioned above can hang on for a long time before being dislodged, making hemlock an example of both the rule and the exception. And then, of course, there's the sugar maple.

The sugar maple readily sprouts in its own shade and can, under favorable conditions (good soil, seed tree nearby), also sprout in the sun. A grove of long-lived sugar maples can dominate a hillside for centuries until death from old age, at which point the next generation of sugar maples is already sprouted and ready to take over. This is part of the reason why sugarbushes can produce maple sugar for generations on end. (The other is that sugarmakers prune out the less-sweet interlopers.)

So why haven't all the rich side slopes in New England been taken over by maple trees, if they persist where others fail? Under most conditions, they don't sprout as readily in the sun as their competitors. Sooner or later, when you're talking centuries, a gust of wind will blow down a few trees, a hurricane will level a hillside, someone wielding an axe or saw will create a clearing, or the sugarbush will be abandoned. Then the sun-sprouters will march back in. Like white birch. Back to the beginning: what you see isn't what you'll get. ∽

A Salmon in Need of Directions

David Deen

Fifty years ago, the Connecticut River was called the best-landscaped sewer in New England. The river could not support aquatic life, and people could not use it to boat, swim, or fish. But since the passage of the Clean Water Act in 1972, the major direct sources of pollution have been reduced, and the river has taken on renewed life. Thanks to this cleanup, we have been able to start restoring anadromous fish to the Connecticut River.

Anadromous fish are all those that return from salt water to fresh water in order to spawn. In the Connecticut, the primary anadromous species are the American shad, the gizzard shad, the blueback herring, the alewife, and—the poster child—the Atlantic salmon. When dams were built across the Connecticut River for power, logging, and transportation, beginning in the 1800s, these species were inadvertently fenced out of the upper river.

The effort to restore anadromous fish to the Connecticut River began in earnest two decades ago. Since the start of the restoration program, the first five dams upriver from Long Island Sound have been modified to allow fish to swim by. There is now a "fish lift" elevator at the dam in Holyoke, Massachusetts, and fish ladders at the dams at Turners Falls, Massachusetts, and at the Vernon, Bellows Falls, and Wilder dams between New Hampshire and Vermont.

Abandoned dams on the smaller tributaries of the Connecticut are also being removed to give migrating fish (both anadromous and resident) access to their preferred spawning habitat. These smaller dams cause water temperature to increase and dissolved oxygen to decrease, making life difficult or impossible for fish and other aquatic species. Many of these dams no longer provide economic benefits yet still do environmental harm, so their removal is a top priority of the restoration program.

The dam at Holyoke, Massachusetts, is where the official fish counting and tagging takes place these days. Holyoke is the first dam on the Connecticut upriver from Long Island Sound (Windsor Locks in Connecticut was breached more than 20 years ago). Forty-seven Atlantic salmon made it over the Holyoke dam in 2003. But salmon are not the only anadromous fish returning to their historic range. In 2003, American shad—288,000 of them—also made it up the

Connecticut River past the dam at Holyoke, along with more than 1,300 blueback herring and 850 gizzard shad.

Shad numbers have increased more than thirtyfold since the restoration program began, in part because shad were never wiped out in the lower reaches of the river. Shad lay their eggs in the river's main channel, and hence a population, albeit reduced, has always lived below the first dam. These native fish ascended the fish ladders and returned to the upper river as soon as they were given the chance.

Salmon, on the other hand, lay their eggs only in the rocky shallows of the upper river and its tributaries. When dams blocked their access to these areas, the salmon were extirpated from the river. New salmon had to be brought in from Maine at the start of the restoration program, and because the Connecticut is the southernmost river in the Atlantic salmon's habitat, it will take time for the Maine genetic stock to become acquainted with the new surroundings.

Also making the trip over the Holyoke dam in 2003 were some 54,000 sea lamprey—a species no one likes to talk about. Sea lamprey do not harm fish in the Connecticut River, however, because, like all true anadromous fish, they do not feed once they return to fresh water. But lamprey have developed a sinister reputation over in Lake Champlain, where they were introduced by humans. The lamprey in Lake Champlain are no longer returning to the sea and are, instead, staying in the lake to feed and grow. They have become a landlocked species and now feed heavily on other fish in the lake.

Back on the Connecticut, of the salmon tagged and released at the Holyoke Dam in 2003, one, it seems, was simply a fish in need of directions. After this particular salmon was tagged and identified in Massachusetts, it was later found back down river at the Rainbow Dam Fishway in Barkhamsted, Connecticut. This fish apparently overshot the Farmington River on its way up the Connecticut, was tagged and released at Holyoke, discovered its "mistake," dropped back down over the Holyoke Dam and downriver to Connecticut, re-entered the Farmington River, and ascended the Rainbow Fishway on its way to its natal spawning area.

As if swimming upstream weren't enough of a challenge by itself! ∽

November

❧

FIRST WEEK

1

If you knock a clubmoss, the yellowish
spores will fly off in little clouds.

Blackberry leaves, deep red-brown, are
now among the best-looking foliage.

Luna moth cocoons, wrapped in
leaves, are on the ground.

The greenness of some mosses and
ferns now stands out: most other
plants are brown-leaved or leafless.

Snow buntings are visiting meadows
on their way to the coast.

Common snipe are hardy birds and will often stay in
meadows until hard freezes force them to fly south.

SECOND WEEK

2

Rattlesnake plantain (really an orchid) stays green
all winter. The leaves are covered with a net
of white veins and grow in a small rosette.

Deer are mating. The gestation period
for whitetails is from 200 to 210 days.

Meadow voles are still breeding.

Look in junipers for cedar waxwings fueling up
on the berries, a large part of their winter diet.

Brook trout are spawning in swift, clean streams.

Deer mice are lining their winter
nests with milkweed fluff.

THIRD WEEK

3

Porcupines are back to eating bark, now
that the leaves have fallen.

Raccoons are settling into winter quarters—a
hollow tree, woodchuck burrow, culvert,
or abandoned building—and will live
off accumulated fat until spring.

Some northern saw-whet owls migrate. After
the first snowfall, those that stay may shift
from hunting redbacked voles in the woods
to hunting meadow voles in open fields.

Until snow covers the fields, waste grain
is an important food for crows.

FOURTH WEEK

4

The redness of highbush cranberries is intensified
when they get a light dusting of snow.

Caterpillars of the cecropia moth, the
largest moth in North America, spin
huge, brown cocoons that incorporate
the twigs of the host tree, weather to
gray, and remain suspended all winter.

Whitetail bucks' antlers are full-grown, and
they begin to spar with one another.

Some ruffed grouse have formed coveys now and
will stay in these small groups through the winter.

October's Witch

~

Virginia Barlow

In late November, after its leaves have changed to a beautiful golden yellow and fallen to the ground, and sometimes even after they have turned sodden from cold rains and no longer crunch crisply underfoot, you may still see the bright yellow flowers of witch hazel, if you are out for a woods walk and luck is with you.

Witch hazel, Latin name *Hamamelis virginiana,* usually begins blooming in October, but it often still has blossoms after everything else in the forest appears to have shut down for the winter. Warm days will bring out just enough late season bees and gnats to pollinate the blossoms, as these insects are eager to top up their store of sugar before intense cold settles in. The flowers are also able to self-pollinate—a good strategy considering the potential for miserable weather in November. Plus, the plant does not go full speed ahead to make seeds. Fertilization of the ovule—the next step, which usually occurs right after pollination—does not take place until spring.

This brings us to another reason to visit witch hazel in autumn: the seedpods. They have been slowly growing fat over the summer and shed their seeds at the same time the flowers are blooming. Though the origin of the name "witch hazel" is disputed and confusing, the Latin name *Hamamelis* is not. It refers to a plant that flowers and fruits at the same time. This is one of the few cases where sitting down to watch seeds leave their seedpods is worthwhile. On the right kind of fall day—dry and a little warmer than the other days—you can hear the popping sounds as witch hazel seed capsules explode, each catapulting two rice-sized shiny black seeds through the understory, sometimes to a distance of 20 or 30 feet. They may lie on the ground for two winters before germinating. Another way to experience this plant version of fireworks is to bring a few branches indoors when they are flowering. The relative warmth and dryness will soon have them popping.

These popping seeds have taken a year to ripen, and the empty capsules will persist on the shrub for most of the following year. Roundish, hairy, and tan, they are a distinctive feature that will help you identify witch hazel in any season. That's another nice thing about it: summer or winter, witch hazel is not like any other shrub. The egg-shaped leaves have nicely scalloped edges—not the confusing sharp-pointed teeth that so many other woody plants have—and the upper surface of the leaf is darker green than usual. With the leaves borne on slender, flattened branches, the plants look like something specially created for the garden and, indeed, many horticultural varieties are available, partly because the arching, layered branches are so appealing.

In the wild, witch hazel is often found in the shady understory of hardwood forests, where it may grow to 25 feet high, though usually it is much shorter. The multiple stems are smooth, becoming scaly with age, and brown; the twigs are zigzag. South of central New England it frequently dominates the understory and can even be an aggressive invader of abandoned fields, so it's good that there's a market for it. In 1866, cutters began delivering witch hazel to Essex, Connecticut, where Thomas Newton Dickinson set up a distillery to manufacture the astringent lotion called witch hazel that has soothed itchy rashes and insect bites ever since. The company still operates from nearby Hamden. The stems are cut in winter, chipped, and distilled to produce an extract that is then mixed with alcohol. After being cut, witch hazel resprouts vigorously, and commercially harvested plants can be whacked to the ground again after five to eight years.

The Dickinson Company now produces more than 2 million gallons of witch hazel extract every year—almost the entire world's supply. Some is sold as the familiar clear liquid used on inflamed skin, but it is also an ingredient in many skin products—from deodorants to soap. Dickinson is said to have gotten the recipe for witch hazel from the Native Americans. They used witch hazel for many of the same skin problems it is used for today.

Though shrubs are generally considered to be short-lived, there is a large, multi-branched witch hazel that still flowers and pops seeds at the Arnold Arboretum in Boston, Massachusetts—it was collected as a young plant in 1883. ❧

Autumn Upside Down

Ted Levin

Lake Fairlee, just in from the Connecticut River on the Vermont side, looks like a giant tadpole, its tail swung north to meet Blood Brook, its head southwest, feeding the unnamed fork of the East Branch of the Ompompanoosuc River.

There is a certain day each autumn, usually in November on 427-acre Lake Fairlee and other large lakes hereabouts, when "fall overturn" takes place—an event not usually marked on human calendars yet absolutely crucial for aquatic life. Without fall overturn, it is quite possible that life on earth would be vastly different from what it is today.

But first, jump back three months. In summer, the waters of Lake Fairlee are stratified into three distinct zones: the top, or epilimnion; the middle, or metalimnion; and the bottom, or hypolimnion. These three zones remain as distinct as oil and vinegar; the winds of summer that agitate the surface do not mix them together. Diving through the epilimnion into the metalimnion is always a shock to any swimmer; the temperature suddenly drops ten to 15° Fahrenheit along an invisible boundary less than 10 feet below the surface.

Of the three layers, the epilimnion—always in contact with the air—is richest in oxygen and lowest in nutrients, which tend to settle to the bottom of the lake. The hypolimnion gains all the nutrients that rain down during the summer, where they become food for the catfish, suckers, and all the decomposers that respire in the sediments.

With the cooler days of autumn, however, the boundaries between the three layers become less distinct. As surface waters cool, they become denser, which causes them to sink in the lake. The warm epilimnion shrinks as the lake gives up heat. If it weren't for a unique property of water, this process would continue until the water at the bottom of the lake reached 32° Fahrenheit and froze. Our ponds and lakes would freeze from the bottom up; fish would perish in lake-size blocks of ice, and human colonization of the Northern Hemisphere would undoubtedly have been greatly slowed.

But water reaches its maximum density not at 32° but at 39.2°. Sometime in November, Lake Fairlee is a nearly uniform 39.2° Fahrenheit, which triggers fall overturn. The slightest wind stirs the lake from top to bottom, distributing nutrients and oxygen through the depths. Life in the lake responds unseen below the surface. Fish normally restricted to the top visit the bottom. Bottom dwellers rise throughout the lake.

As cold autumn weather continues to cool the lake below 39.2° Fahrenheit, the overturn comes to an end. The lake stops circulating. The ever-colder surface water is now less dense than the rest of the lake, and this cooler water floats. Ice finally forms, generally by late December, and the lake is sealed off from the wind.

If fall overturn hadn't already taken place, this skin of ice would be fatal to many animals that depend on the surge of oxygen and nutrients from fall overturn to make it through the long winter ahead.

In the spring, when the ice melts and the lake water warms to a uniform 39.2° Fahrenheit, spring overturn begins. Once more, nutrients and oxygen are distributed throughout the body of water. Then, when April grades into May, the surface of Lake Fairlee warms,

mixing of the waters ceases, and the lake is again stratified into its three distinct layers.

We cannot see overturn happen, of course, but I imagine that the flock of bufflehead I saw last November, which had just arrived from central Canada en route to some mid-Atlantic estuary for a winter respite, found plenty of aquatic insects and small fish dispersed at nearly all depths. Ducks idled in the middle of the lake that day, and when I paddled my kayak toward them, they dove, powered by their large hind feet. Not far off, they surfaced—three males, mostly white, and four dull-colored, either females or young of the year.

With twilight closing in, I turned back north toward Lake Fairlee's public landing. A skittish blue jay bathed, while noisy crows soared above. Four herring gulls and an immature black-legged kittywake—a very rare inland visitor from the Arctic—eddied against a cranberry-colored sky. ∾

The Ecology of the Hunt

Chuck Wooster

We live surrounded by deer. They observe us as we cut wood, walk in the woods, or step out back to hang the laundry. They turn up at the edges of fields, deep in the woods, or in the rough between suburban houses. But for all their abundance, we rarely see them. And except for a few short weeks in November, few of us give deer a second thought.

Deer thrive in our midst because, like us, they are generalists. White-tailed deer are found in all 50 states and all but the most northerly Canadian provinces. They eat a wide range of foods and, also like us, don't necessarily eat what is best for them; although starving deer will invariably choose the most nutritious foods available, well-fed deer have been observed by biologists walking right past healthy food to sample new or unusual treats.

In addition to being generalists, whitetails have a second crucial ability that has contributed to their ecological success: their fertility rate adjusts itself each year to match changes in food availability. If food is plentiful, does will have two or more fawns each spring. If food is scarce and starvation is threatening, does will either not conceive at all, will conceive only one fawn, or will abort one or more fawns before springtime.

All of which brings us to November, the annual period so anticipated by hunters and so dreaded by hunting's opponents. Though much of the hunting debate revolves around guns and gun control, most of the details of the actual hunt are based on the biology and ecology of the deer herd.

For example, hunting season is held in the fall not arbitrarily but for two important reasons. First, fall is "the rut" for deer—the annual mating time during which both does and bucks—but especially bucks—lose their normal wariness and pursue sex at the expense of safety. Bucks in other seasons are often so elusive that even catching a glimpse of one is an unusual occurrence. Hunters armed with the latest in rifle technology would have little chance of shooting a buck in May; as it is, only about one hunter in eight is successful during Vermont's and New Hampshire's autumn hunting seasons.

But hunting season is held in the fall for a second important reason—the more deer that die in the fall, the fewer that are likely to starve in the winter. In the absence of hunting and predation, nearly all deer mortality occurs in the winter when food disappears and shelter is restricted to thick softwood stands. Following particularly harsh winters, deer fecundity is also suppressed since the does have had to endure limited food during the winter.

When deer are removed from the herd by hunters and, more recently, by coyotes, the opposite effect occurs: fewer adults compete for the same food, fertility rises, and more fawns are born in the spring. When hunting, predation, and habitat are all in balance, the deer herd tends to be steady in size, and individual deer tend to be both large and healthy.

The job of balancing all these factors falls to biologists in the state wildlife departments, who monitor the deer herd to determine the rules and regulations of each hunting season. If there are too many deer, individuals become smaller and less healthy, and ground-nesting songbirds (and other species that live in the undergrowth) suffer as deer eat everything in sight—including carefully tended flower beds. Biologists attempt to reduce the herd by lengthening the hunting season, increasing the number of deer that each hunter can shoot, and allowing does to be killed along with bucks.

And if there are too few deer? Only once in thousands of years has this happened—during the great sheep boom of the nineteenth century when market hunting of venison was legal and most of our forests were leveled for

pasture and lumber. Of these two factors, the loss of habitat was the most significant; deer can recover from heavy predation if adequate food is available, but they cannot rebound if they have neither food nor shelter during the critical winter months.

But wouldn't deer be better off if we just left them alone? Anthropologist Richard Nelson, whose book *Heart and Blood: Living With Deer in America* should be in the hands of everyone who loves deer, hunter or not, reminds us of our history. "Humans have likely been the most important predators on deer for thousands of years. We ourselves—and the hunger in our bellies—may have influenced the evolutionary sculpting of this creature. Selective pressure from human hunting would have favored traits such as acute senses, secretiveness, wariness and escape behaviors, camouflaging coloration, cryptic patterns of body movement, and fleetness of foot."

In short, deer are what they are because of us. And we because of them. ᴄᴏ

Rotten Luck: On-Site Recycling

Dan Lambert

The autumn wind and rain have stripped the hardwoods of their leaves, exposing the messy innards of our forests. From the roadside, travelers can glimpse a rotten stump poking up through the leaf litter, an aspen snapped in two over a stone wall, or the crown of a hemlock trailing in the stream that washed away its footing. White birch branches lie scattered like bones in the shade of longer-lived species. Roots that once traced dark passages through the soil point accusingly at the sky.

It may seem a waste to allow a tree to succumb to competition, old age, disease, or extreme weather. It offends our Yankee sensibility to stand by as it collapses and disappears into the duff without having framed a house, fed a woodstove, or supplied a paper mill. Yet it is the very process of decay that ensures the vitality of the forest overall, providing countless benefits to plants, wildlife, and people.

Standing dead trees, called snags, and other coarse woody debris (CWD) provide foraging opportunities, shelter, and travel-ways for wildlife. Decomposing wood also plays a significant role in maintaining animal, plant, and soil productivity, with the material's size, position, and stage of decay determining the contribution of CWD to the forest's health.

The diverse organisms that inhabit snags make certain that nothing goes to waste. Dead wood harbors a thriving community of fungi, bacteria, and wood-destroying critters such as bark beetles, borers, sawyers, and carpenter ants. Woodpeckers feed on these insects, and the nest cavities excavated by woodpeckers are re-used by owls, tree swallows, wood ducks, and squirrels for nesting and breeding. Chickadees and nuthatches, cavity-nesters themselves, find shelter in snags on frigid winter nights.

On summer days, woodland bats dangle from their feet in tree hollows and beneath strips of sloughing bark. A grove of flaking snags with southern or southwestern exposure may provide a warm microclimate for a bat maternity colony. In such a grove, brown creepy bats could find themselves jockeying for space with bona fide brown creepers, diminutive songbirds that nest behind loose bark. They might also encounter competition from chimney swifts, which nest in open-topped snags and resemble bats in their aerial foraging behavior.

When a snag starts to break apart and fall to the ground, it adds structure to the understory in the form of stumps, leaning stems, downed branches, and sometimes upturned root systems. Each of these features presents an opportunity for one species or another. Chicken-of-the-woods sprout from decaying stumps in a wrinkly, fanlike form. This fungus is edible when cooked, unlike deadly Galerina and wolf's milk slime mold, two other decomposers that colonize stumps but bear less-appetizing names.

Leaning stems provide white-footed mice and ermine access to food and cover in the upper layers of the forest canopy. Together with downed branches, fallen stems serve as runways over stone walls, across streams, and beneath the snow. The root balls of toppled trees feature nooks and crannies that shelter winter wren and yellow-bellied flycatcher nests. But for cover and concealment, rotten logs take the prize.

Anyone who has turned over a log in an advanced stage of decay has discovered a cool, moist refuge, safe from the extremes of heat, drought, and even low-intensity fires. Occupants of this niche include tree-supporting mycorrhizal fungi, worms, sow bugs, and the most abundant terrestrial vertebrate in New England, the red-backed salamander. Studies conducted in hardwoods of New Hampshire and New York have shown that this four-inch amphibian accounts for more biomass per acre than any other vertebrate. Females of the species suspend grapelike egg clusters from the bottom of decaying logs or from the roof of a small cavity within the log.

Just as animal life begins beneath and within logs, plant life springs forth on top. Mosses and liverworts carpet spongy logs, gaining advantage from the moisture and steady release of nutrients. Yellow birch seedlings also flourish on "nurse logs." Stilt-like roots on older

birches provide evidence of this regeneration strategy.

If you care for your own woods, resist the urge to tidy up. Instead, ensure a continuous supply of snags and CWD in various stages of decay. Although a variety of CWD is important, keep in mind that larger material lasts longer, holds more moisture, and will be used by more organisms over the course of its decomposition. When cutting trees, avoid disturbing or damaging fallen logs and be sure to retain a few snags. Delimb, top, and buck trees on site, so as to leave CWD scattered throughout the woods rather than concentrated at landings. Finally, retain any windthrow on steep slopes and in riparian areas to stabilize soil, control runoff, and guarantee a long-term, moderate supply of CWD to streams. By following these guidelines, you will achieve a true Yankee woodlot, where nothing goes to waste. ∿

Has the Golden Ghost Returned?

Cathi Buni

Leslie Bowen and her husband, Myron, keep track of 350 cattle, 28 horses, 30 pigs, and 120 chickens on their farm in Rochester, Vermont. For almost a year, Bowen has also been on the trail of what she says is a mountain lion.

She's seen mountain lions before, Bowen says, in northern Arizona, where she lived for two years before moving to Vermont. Bowen says she has no doubt about what she saw on North View Drive one morning in March of 2003.

"It stood between knee- and hip-high, was tawny colored, had a big head, and that very long, thick, graceful tail," she says. "It sort of looked at me for a few seconds, and then, very casually, slipped into the woods."

Since then, Bowen and at least six neighbors say they've seen a mountain lion. Coming out of a barn full of horses. Passing through drivers' headlights. Watching a child play basketball.

Felis concolor—an unspotted cat known variously as cougar, puma, mountain lion, panther, and, here in New England, catamount, from cat-of-the-mountains—once roamed North America from coast to coast. But by the beginning of the 1900s, extensive logging and relentless hunting of what had become accepted as a dangerous pest had taken a toll on *F. concolor cougar,* the eastern subspecies of mountain lion. While the lion continued to survive on bigger lands out West, the cats seemingly disappeared from northern New England.

Catamounts are not particularly fussy about where they live. They require 5 to 25 square miles to roam but reportedly live quite contentedly on the outskirts of Californian and Coloradan suburbs. Despite news of mauled joggers and babies in these states, we're more likely to die from a bee sting than in the jaws of a catamount, an animal that prefers deer and sometimes beaver or wild turkey, none of which is in short supply here in the Vermont and New Hampshire. According to the U.S. Fish & Wildlife Service, mountain lions will occasionally eat domestic livestock, "when available." Nobody argues that Vermont wouldn't make a perfectly suitable hangout for catamounts. And why not Rochester?

Vermont's Fish & Wildlife Department has recorded an average of 38 sightings a year for the last 10 years. Here's the rub. In the hundred-plus years that have passed since 1881, when Alexander Crowell shot and killed a mountain lion in Barnard, only one sighting has been proven with hard evidence.

And that was back in 1994, after a man named Mark Walker spotted a mother catamount and two cubs in Craftsbury. Scat bagged soon after was sent off to the U.S. Fish & Wildlife Service's forensic lab in Oregon, which a few months later confirmed that the sample contained the hair of a mountain lion.

What couldn't be determined, and what remains the center of considerable debate, is where Vermont's mystery cats might be coming from. Catamounts are solitary, shy, and elusive; their very survival is based on an ability to remain unseen and unheard while stalking prey. No small feat for an animal that, as a yearling, might well weigh 90 pounds.

They could be part of a remnant population that, by sticking through the tough times, is thriving in regenerated forests bursting with white-tailed deer. They could be coming down from the remote reaches of Canada or northern Maine. Or, as some speculate about the coyote in the 1950s, perhaps they're making a generations-long migration from out West.

Then again, Vermont's cats may not be wild at all but commercially bred animals escaped from their cages or released by tired owners or even wildlife activists looking to accelerate a cougar reintroduction. Doug Blodgett, the Vermont Fish & Wildlife Department biologist who followed up on Leslie Bowen's call, repeatedly emphasizes how cheaply and easily you or I could buy a catamount over the Internet. "Two thousand bucks and you, too, could own a cougar," he says.

Back on North Hollow Farm in Rochester, the Bowens watch over their cattle, which, Bowen reports, have taken to circling instinctively around their young at even the slightest disruption. The tracks she cast and the scat sample she bagged at the request of the Vermont Fish & Wildlife Department both have been tested and identified as "canine." But Bowen says she knows it's a catamount out there. Says Blodgett, "We just don't have the resources to follow up on all these sightings."

When asked about the catamount's ghostlike visitations, Susan Morse, a forestry and wildlife consultant and founder of Huntington-based Keeping Track, says, "The only answer to the question of whether catamounts are here in Vermont is that no one knows for sure." ∽

Wood Warms You Twice, Not Thrice

Chuck Wooster

The other day, I was loading the last of the firewood into the woodshed when a friend stopped by. "Looks like fun," he said. I happened to know that he himself was not a wood burner, and, judging from the tone in his voice, I gathered he had not become one since our last meeting. So I skipped the usual blather about the virtues and advantages of wood burning and went straight for the jugular.

"Burning wood doesn't add to global warming," I said, knowing full well that he considered himself something of an environmentalist and was loath to be outflanked on the issue. So off we went.

A common misconception is that, because carbon dioxide in the atmosphere causes global warming, and because burning wood adds carbon dioxide to the atmosphere, burning wood, therefore, also contributes to global warming. But that's not so. From a chemical perspective, all carbon dioxide is created equal. But from an ecological perspective, the source of the carbon dioxide is all important.

Global warming is being caused by "the greenhouse effect"—a description of the dual role that carbon dioxide plays in regulating our climate. Much like the panes of glass in a greenhouse, carbon dioxide lets in more of the sun's energy than it lets out. Light tends to pass through while heat tends to be trapped. Adding more carbon dioxide to the atmosphere is akin to adding more layers of glass to the greenhouse—the temperature inside goes up.

But what if, instead of adding more panes to the greenhouse roof, you were simply swapping one pane for another? Putting one up and taking one off? The temperature inside would not rise. And that's the case with burning wood.

The carbon found in wood (and, indeed, in every living thing) is part of the earth's biosphere, that combination of the earth's crust and atmosphere where organisms live. Carbon in the biosphere is continually cycling between the air and the earth—entering the atmosphere as carbon dioxide when an old tree decays (or is burned) and being removed from the atmosphere as a tree grows and incorporates the carbon into new wood. Burning firewood for heat fits into this ongoing cycle and is, therefore, akin to swapping glass panes on the greenhouse roof—we add some carbon dioxide to the atmosphere during burning and we subtract some as the woodlot regrows. But there is no net increase.

This is particularly true in our corner of the world, where tree growth has exceeded tree harvesting for the last century and a half. As upland fields and farms have reverted to forest since the end of the Civil War, for every tree cut down to heat our houses in Vermont and New Hampshire, more than one has grown in to take its place.

The carbon found in fossil fuels, on the other hand, is not part of the biosphere and is not part of this biological carbon cycle. Fossil fuel carbon was locked up in the crust several hundred million years ago at a time when there was far more carbon dioxide in the atmosphere than there is today (and when the earth's temperature was significantly warmer than it is today). Removing this carbon from the ground and releasing it into the air is causing a net gain of carbon dioxide in the atmosphere and slowly returning us to those prehistoric (and less hospitable) conditions. Only if we could remove this extra carbon from the atmosphere and somehow inject it back into the ground could we burn fossil fuels without increasing the earth's temperature.

Take the example of a juggler who is managing to keep a dozen tennis balls in the air. Suddenly a bystander starts lobbing additional tennis balls into the ring. Eventually, the juggler can't keep up and starts dropping the balls. It isn't the tennis balls themselves that are causing the problem, it's the *extra* tennis balls. Similarly, it isn't carbon dioxide molecules (the tennis balls) that are causing global warming, it's the *extra* carbon dioxide molecules lobbed in from burning fossil fuels. The carbon dioxide molecules released from burning firewood are already part of the juggler's original dozen.

Back at my woodshed, I'm pleased to say that my friend and I parted on good terms, though he did become distracted during the conversation, and I believe he ended up stacking more of my wood than he had intended. Afterward, I realized that Henry Thoreau had it only half right when, writing at the dawn of the fossil fuel age, he pointed out that wood warms you twice: once while you're burning it and once while you're putting it up. He forgot to mention that it won't warm you a third time. ∽

December

❧

FIRST WEEK

1

The evergreen leaves of goldthread can form a large,
dark green carpet, though each plant is quite tiny.

Inside a honeybee hive, it's warm and cozy.
The metabolic heat of bees fanning their
wings, fueled by stored honey, keeps the
indoor temperature nearly constant.

Yard evergreens should be watered
thoroughly before the soil freezes.

The white-crowned sparrows that stop at
your feeder may remember it and stop again in
spring. These hardy birds breed in the far North.

SECOND WEEK

2

A frozen apple stuffed into the crotch of a tree
is the work of a red squirrel. It will reclaim its
cache when deep snow covers the ground.

Sweet cicely sprouts new leaves in autumn. It
stays green all winter, ready to enlarge quickly
in spring before tree leaves intercept the light.

In winter, the screech owl's diet shifts from
insect-rich fare to small mammals and birds:
juncos, sparrows, and even mourning doves.
These low-flying owls frequently collide with cars.

THIRD WEEK

The berries of wild roses that persist into winter are high on the list of food for mammals and birds.

Look in birches for pine siskins, often in flocks of 50 to 100 birds. They chitter in whispers as they feed.

Evergreen wood fern and Christmas fern in the woods and rock polypody on rocky outcrops show up when the snow is not too deep. These species stay green all winter.

Mice will move indoors after a heavy snow. Considering their size, they make a lot of noise.

FOURTH WEEK

New seed catalogs arrive in the mail. Next year's gardening season is in the planning stage.

After the first deep snow, deer will head for deeryards, usually south- or west-facing slopes with dense softwood cover.

Snow usually does not deter moose: their long, skinny legs can plow through 30 inches of it without a problem.

On cold nights, grouse will dig themselves deep into the snow. It may be as much as 50° Fahrenheit warmer beneath a good, thick blanket of snow

Sugar Maples Beat the Cold

Ted Levin

I want to know the secrets of the sugar maples in our woods. I want to know how they survive the winter, naked except for their thin robes of grooved bark. I want to know how they survive the winter when the earth turns to stone and the wind drives needles of ice and snow. And I want to know how next spring's sensitive new buds, encased in a coif of soft brown scales, survive more than three months of on-again, off-again sub-zero weather.

Like a sweater, bark is our maples' first line of defense against the cold. Bark consists of two distinct groups of cells: those alive (the inner bark) and those not (the outer bark). The secondary phloem, conduit for transporting the maple's food, is synonymous with inner bark. Each year, as our maples add a new growth ring, a foamy layer of old phloem is pushed to the outside. These cells die. The foam hardens into fatty, waxy substances filled with capsules of air and becomes the bark we see that is exposed to the weather. This outer bark provides some protection from sudden changes in temperature.

But not much. A tree, after all, is not heated from within, and since trees are more than 60 percent water, avoiding internal ice dam-

age is a maple's biggest winter challenge. How do they do it? The answer is that they rely on water's ability to supercool.

At −36.6° Fahrenheit, ice will form spontaneously in pure, distilled water. As long as there are no dust particles to serve as nuclei for ice crystals, pure water will remain ice-free until that very low temperature. Our northern trees make a point of keeping their internal water as pure as possible, and hence they can reach −36.6° before freezing. In fact, the northern ranges of sugar maple, American beech, and yellow birch correspond roughly with the isotherm that indicates a winter minimum temperature of −40°. Beech actually endures a low of −42, sugar maple −45, and yellow birch −49.

These slight differences in cold tolerance are attributed to the antifreeze properties of the respective trees' intracellular sugars. A hike up Mount Washington or Mount Mansfield quickly confirms this, as first beech and then sugar maple cease to grow. Yellow birch, the hardiest of the three, grows all the way up into the lower end of the spruce and fir zone, an ambassador from another realm.

But pure water and antifreeze aren't the only tricks up our maples' sleeves. In August, maples produce abscisic acid, a growth-inhibiting hormone that also increases the permeability of their cell membranes. With the first light frosts of September, the trees' living cells begin to release water into the empty spaces between cells. When a hard freeze hits, ice crystals will form in these intercellular spaces, while the unfrozen water inside the cells' cytoplasm continues to migrate toward the frozen water outside the cell wall. As more water leaves, the living cells shrivel like deflated balloons, further increasing the concentration of dissolved solids within the cell walls. And the higher the concentration of dissolved solids, the lower the freezing point.

Ice crystals sometimes rupture the outer, stiff cell wall, indenting but not puncturing the inner, elastic plasma membrane. If the bottom should fall out of the mercury, however, and temperatures drop below the maple's −45° threshold, as often happens on the cutting edge of the tree's northern range, ice will form inside the cells. When the plasma membrane ruptures, the cell dies. When too many cells die, the tree dies.

Acid rain is making it more difficult for some trees to withstand cold because acidity strips calcium from the soil and calcium is essential for the proper functioning of cell membranes. Studies on red spruce have found a reduced cold hardiness among trees growing on calcium-depleted soils and among trees whose needles are exposed to acidic fog and clouds throughout the winter.

Some northern trees go one step further and nearly freeze-dry their cells by removing almost all their cellular water until huge crystalline masses of ice crowd the intercellular spaces. The paper birch and red osier dogwood that pepper our wetlands can survive submersion in liquid nitrogen at −321° and still recover upon thawing.

With the unlocking of spring, intercellular ice melts, water is sucked back into the maples' cells (and, perhaps, into a waiting sap bucket), and normal metabolic processes resume. At this point, surprisingly, the trees have lost their cold hardiness, and even a minor spring freeze can damage them. Trees that withstood twenty-five below in January can be severely damaged at twenty-five above in May. ∽

A Thief of Stars

Madeline Bodin

There it was, a faint orange glow in the northern sky. Could it be, at long last, the northern lights? I stared at the glow while the cold night air nipped at my cheeks. The light seemed awfully uniform and was not moving. Weren't the northern lights supposed to be mostly green anyway? Or if orange, not this dull shade?

That dull shade of orange was familiar. I had seen it before, but always near cities. It wasn't the northern lights, but "skyglow," the reflection of electric lights, usually street lights, into the night sky. I never expected to see skyglow from my back porch in rural Vermont, but light pollution—and skyglow is just one form of it—is an increasing problem, not just in cities, but in rural areas like ours.

"Twenty years ago, one could actually see the Milky Way in Manchester (New Hampshire)," says Mike Pelletier of the New Hampshire Citizens for Responsible Lighting (NHCRL). "Now, one cannot see it, and several major constellations have also been replaced in the night sky by an orange glow."

But light pollution is not just skyglow. When your neighbor's security light shines in your eyes when you are trying to sleep, that's "light trespass," another form of light pollu-

tion. Glare is another light pollution problem that can happen anywhere there is an electric light. If the light is poorly aimed and shines in your eyes, that's glare, and it's particularly dangerous when you are driving.

Skyglow is not limited to cities as large as Manchester. Mike Stebbins, a NHCRL member, says that Conway, New Hampshire, has massive skyglow, and Claremont, New Hampshire is getting there. Other New Hampshire cities with notable skyglow are Keene and Tilton. In the Upper Valley region of the twin states, Hanover, Lebanon, and White River Junction produce notable skyglow. In Vermont, there is skyglow not only from cities such as Burlington and Rutland but also from smaller towns such as Randolph and Morrisville. Tiny Ludlow, Vermont, appears to be the source of the skyglow in my backyard.

It's not that outdoor lighting is bad. We need lights so we don't back into other cars in parking lots, so we feel safe walking at night, and to keep burglars away from our homes. It is possible, however, to do all those things without robbing the sky of its darkness.

In 1996, the Chittenden County Regional Planning Commission in Vermont published a booklet that's still considered one of the most understandable explanations of light pollution around. While you may not want to curl up with it in front of the fire, in a mere 48 pages it tells you everything you need to know about outdoor lighting, including how a town can be safe and well lit while saving energy and eliminating light pollution. For example, to reduce skyglow and glare, one solution is using "full cutoff" fixtures that prevent light from shining above the horizontal.

Stargazers are usually the first to notice light pollution, but it affects other living things, too. Sea turtles are drawn inland by electric lights instead of toward the ocean after hatching. Every year, thousands of migrating songbirds crash into lighted skyscrapers or lit communications towers and die.

Thanks to our mountains, Vermont and New Hampshire have fewer towers that are over 199 feet tall than other parts of the country. That height is important because at 200 feet federal law requires a light on top of the tower for aviation safety. While communications towers themselves cause some problems for birds, it's the lights on the towers that seem to cause the most casualties.

The worst cases seem to be foggy nights, nights with low clouds in spring or autumn, and towers lit with steady or pulsing red lights. Night migrating songbirds are sometimes unable to leave the lit area. They circle the tower, creating a whirlwind of birds. They may crash into the tower, guy wires, each other, or fall from the sky exhausted. While all species of migrating songbirds are vulner-

able to this fate, thrushes, vireos, and warblers appear to be the most vulnerable.

Two years ago, the U.S. Fish & Wildlife Department published a set of guidelines for communications towers, which included advice on light. White lights are better than red. Strobe lights are better than steady lights, and the flashes should be as few and as far between as allowed by the Federal Aviation Administration.

Light pollution steals the stars from the sky (or at least our view of them) and the birds from the air. It creeps up on us under good intentions, but is a thief just the same. We can bring back the darkness of night with simple techniques, consistently applied. We need only to notice and care. ∽

Shrew or Mole? Mouse or Vole?

Michael Caduto

When it comes to nature, we tend to stuff things we don't know into pigeonholes that are already defined by the familiar. If someone tells me their cat has left a "present" of a dead "mouse" on the doorstep, I ask the usual questions: How big is it? What color is the fur? How long is its tail? What size are the eyes and ears? How pointed is its nose? Chances are that it's not a mouse.

Often, here in northern New England, the deceased is a 4- to 5-inch-long northern short-tailed shrew, with its dark gray fur, inch-long tail, pinpoint eyes, sharp nose, fur-covered ears, and stubby legs bearing sharp claws for digging. And the cat is not necessarily leaving the shrew as a gift: short-taileds have glands on the hips and belly that emit such a strong, musky odor that most predators can't stomach the idea of eating one. Snakes and owls actually partake of the pungent, as do other shrews, which have a poor olfactory sense.

With a metabolism that is 60 times the rate of a human's, shrews are more often the predator than the prey. Wielding sharp teeth, short-tailed shrews can consume more than their own weight each day, so they are not fussy about whom or what they eat. In-sects, worms, and spiders are fair game, as are centipedes and salamanders. Meadow voles are a popular item on the menu, along with mice, snakes, small rabbits, the hatchlings of ground-nesting birds, and even other shrews. Unique among mammals, the bite of a short-tailed shrew contains a poison that can paralyze and even kill its prey.

As they tunnel, short-tailed shrews navigate like bats and dolphins: they emit ultrasonic clicks that reflect back to their ears to create an aural picture of the surroundings. From as far as 2 feet away, a short-tailed shrew's echo-location helps it to find solid objects, holes, and places where grass may block a runway. Their sixth sense may even serve to identify predators and prey.

When the north wind blows, the short-tailed shrew's short summer coat grows longer and turns a darker shade of gray, making it appear very mole-like. But moles are larger and more robust insectivores with powerful front shoulders and outsized front feet and claws. The star-nosed mole has a 3-inch-long tail and an unmistakable sunburst-shaped nose bearing 22 pink rays that encircle the tip. Another species of local mole, the hairy-tailed mole, is about 6 inches long. They have a short, furry tail, and their backs are covered with fur that ranges from dark gray to black. Each day, one of these feisty, 2-ounce critters can eat more than its own weight in earthworms, snails, millipedes, slugs, and insects. Its winter tunnels lie 10 to 20 inches beneath the surface.

The short-tailed shrew most closely resembles yet another species, the meadow vole, but voles are tawny brown in summer, turn grayer in winter, have a blunt nose and a tail that ranges from 1½–2½ inches long. They have beady black eyes, short round ears, and chunky bodies that measure 6–7½ inches with the tail. Voles tunnel below the surface and create runways in the thick grass. Their food includes grass, seeds, grains, and tubers. Mice are blamed for much of the damage done by voles, which eat prodigious amounts of roots, countless flower bulbs, and are so fond of bark that they often girdle and kill young shrubs and trees. And meadow voles can produce up to 17 litters each year!

If you look carefully at short-tailed shrews, moles, and voles, they don't resemble mice, which have large, prominent eyes, big ears, and tails about as long as their bodies. Our two common species are the white-footed mouse and deer mouse. White-footed mice are reddish brown, with a dark patch running along the back. Deer mice have brownish-gray fur and are nearly 7–8½ inches long, including the 3- to 4-inch-long tail. Mice eat as much as a third of their weight in food each day, including lots of seeds, grains, nuts, and fruits. A third or more of their diet consists of animal foods such as small insects, grubs, and worms. They cache sizeable stores of food as autumn days grow short.

When a wintering "mouse" appears in one of the live traps I set in our porous, Civil-War-era house, I look closely. Shrew? (Sharp nose, short legs and tail.) Mole? (Big shoulders, claws, and a longer tail.) Vole? (Brown, big, blunt nose.) Mouse? (Big ears and eyes, very long tail.) I handle them carefully on our journey of at least 2 miles, the minimum distance from which they won't later return. And I am especially careful when moving a shrew so as to avoid its painful, toxic bite. ～

DEER MOUSE

MEADOW VOLE

HAIRY·TAILED MOLE

SHORT·TAILED SHREW

Freezing Frogs

~

Tii McLane

It was a busy summer in the pond at the foot of my hill. Hundreds of wood frogs mated there. I watched their eggs hatch, watched as tadpoles grew up, got legs, lost tails, and headed for the woods for which they are named. There, I assume, they spent the summer and fall fattening up on insects. But where are they now that there is no more food to be found and ice and snow have covered the ground?

Some frog species burrow into the mud at the bottom of the pond, insulating themselves against freezing air temperatures, but wood frogs have evolved a different strategy. They accept a frozen fate by digging down into a couple of inches of leaf litter.

Samuel Hearne, journeying in the Arctic in 1769–1772, described them: "Frogs of various colours are numerous in those parts as far North as the latitude 61 degrees. . . . I have frequently seen them dug up with the moss, frozen as hard as ice; in which state the legs are as easily broken off as a pipe-stem . . . but by wrapping them in warm skins, and exposing them to a slow fire, they soon recover life." He was likely referring to our wood frog, *Rana sylvatica,* found both in the Arctic and here in northern New England.

Although the wood frog has been the most extensively studied, other amphibians also possess this ability to tolerate freezing: the gray tree frog, spring peeper, and chorus frog, along with one species of Siberian salamander, the immature spotted turtle, the eastern box turtle, the pond-slider turtle, and the garter snake, as well as numerous invertebrates.

As you can imagine, freezing is tough on most creatures. Ice crystals damage cells, causing them to rupture and collapse. Toxins build up in cells and cause nervous system dysfunction. Increased heart rates and damage due to rapid cooling are also potential hazards that could lead to death.

This does not seem to intimidate the wood frog, which, unlike humans in the Northeast, does very little to prepare for the long cold winter. The single preparation this frog makes is to store glycogen in its liver. In the fall, these animals may harbor 2–10 times more of this substance than pond-hibernating species.

Once temperatures drop below freezing, and water just inside the skin of the frog starts to freeze, the wood frog rapidly transforms this glycogen into glucose, which serves as antifreeze. Blood glucose can increase up to 200-fold in response to freezing. Besides manufacturing antifreeze, freeze-tolerant frogs are able to evacuate water from major organs, thus reducing the formation of ice in these critical areas. (Some plants have a similar ability to protect sensitive tissue.) Up to 65 percent of the frog's body-water in the intercellular spaces can freeze without causing damage. The glucose, meanwhile, keeps the water remaining inside the cells from freezing.

One strange twist in the process is that as water turns to ice, heat is given off, and it is this heat that saves the frogs from cooling too rapidly. They can freeze, but they mustn't freeze too fast.

Frozen dissected frogs appear dead. There is no sign of breathing or blood flow. Organs appear bloodless. Heartbeats are absent or intermittent. If there is a midwinter thaw (or, in the case of Samuel Hearne, warm skins and a blazing fire), glucose levels subside and the frog thaws. The organs with the highest glucose levels (liver, heart, kidney) thaw first, allowing metabolism to start back up. This process can fluctuate back and forth throughout the winter. Because thawing is slower than freezing, and because there is usually a nice thick blanket of insulating snow, the frogs are not likely to thaw many times during the winter.

The temperature to which frogs freeze and the length of time they remain frozen is crucial. One hundred percent will survive frozen to −1.5° Celsius for 14 days, but only 50 percent will survive at this same temperature for 28 days. None will survive temperatures as low as −30° Celsius. A cold winter

with no snow, therefore, is devastating to the local wood frog population.

It is not clear why some frogs have evolved this freezing strategy. Maybe there is some danger that lurks for them under the protection of an ice-covered pond, leading them to choose a different winter home. Or maybe they couldn't stomach the idea of being trapped under a foot of ice all winter with a bunch of bull frogs. Either way, they have what it took to develop the mechanisms needed to withstand freezing. ∼

The Coyote is Here to Stay

Ted Levin

One recent winter morning, when I awoke at dawn and glanced out our bedroom window, a nervous coyote slipped from the woods—crouching, tail tight between its hind legs like a naughty dog—and walked tentatively to my mammal feeding station in the side yard. The coyote stood for some time, eyes fixed on the woods, before he gathered the courage to chisel bits of meat from the rock-hard deer carcass. Grabbing my binoculars, I hurried downstairs for an eye-level look.

What manner of beast is the coyote? It is the most adaptable, the most intelligent, the most resourceful wild animal in our area, if not all of America. Not only is the coyote a functioning part of the wild Northeast but it has also redefined the roles of many other animals. The coyote eats deer and wild turkey, yet both species thrive. The coyote doesn't eat red fox or bobcat, yet both predators suffer in its presence. It communes with ravens and train whistles and sirens, and its yipping falsetto gives meaning to a winter night. As a recent immigrant to Vermont, the coyote is neither predictable nor sacred and is blamed for everything but the weather.

Before Europeans carved up the eastern forests and the heartland prairies, the coyote was more or less confined to desert and scrubland. It either lived in regions that did not support a population of gray wolves, or it lived furtively in the landscape cracks between adjacent wolf packs. Once the East had been cleared and grasslands plowed, wolves were virtually exterminated. Then, coyotes began to make a bold and innovative move eastward.

On October 24, 1944, a fox hunter in Holderness, New Hampshire, shot a coyote, the first ever recorded in New England. Four years later, one went down in Vermont. By the 1960s, coyotes had become established in northern New England, and by the 1990s, a few individuals began appearing in seemingly unlikely corners of the Northeast: downtown Boston and Central Park in New York City. Today, Vermont supports between 3,000 and 4,000 coyotes in the summer. After mortality and dispersal have taken a toll, the population shrinks to between 1,500 and 2,000 during the winter.

Eastern coyotes are much more secretive than their western cousins. They prefer the woods to the meadows, the night to the day, and do not as often broadcast their exuberance.

Once the day began to lighten, my side-yard coyote hitched his tail between his legs and slunk back into the woods. In his absence, a pair of ravens, which had been visiting the carcass for the past several days, flew in to feed. According to Bernd Heinrich, University of Vermont biologist and author of *Ravens in Winter*, ravens circling high above a carcass often alert coyotes to the imminent possibility of food; if a carcass is unopened, feeding coyotes chew through the hide, which provides an access point for hungry ravens. In turn, ravens cache pieces of meat, which coyotes often track down and consume.

Fifteen minutes after a pair of ravens appeared on the carcass, a gray fox drove them off. The fox seemed unconcerned that the scent of a coyote littered the area; it fed in daylight and even napped in the open. Although gray foxes appear to be holding their own, eastern coyotes have had a profound impact on red foxes, killing them or driving them out of their home ranges, forcing them to live in the narrow zones between adjacent coyote packs, much the same way wolves pinch the range of coyotes. The opposing fates of the two foxes appear to be a byproduct of species-specific behavior. When threatened, a gray fox climbs a tree or hides in a burrow. A red fox runs. And coyotes run faster.

Eastern coyotes have also displaced bobcats, though not by running them down. Coyotes, by virtue of their catholic feeding habits, are much more common than bobcats, which are strictly carnivores. Before settlement, wolves and catamounts stole prey from bobcats. In the absence of the big predators, Vermont's bobcat population peaked by the 1930s and 1940s. Since the arrival of the carcass-stealing coyote, bobcat numbers have been in decline.

Make no mistake about it, the eastern coyote is a predator; it kills fawns in the spring and early summer and adult deer in the winter, particularly in deep snow. Faced with several thousand hungry coyotes, however, Vermont's deer herd has steadily grown since the early 1980s. In fact, I believe deer need an effective predator—wolves for instance—to help control their numbers. Until the wolves return or are returned to Vermont and New Hampshire, however, I'll enjoy my chance encounters with the eastern coyotes—survivalist extraordinaire. ༄

Does Frost Really Crack Trees?

Michael Snyder

Most people tend to call any crack in a tree trunk a "frost crack." But then, most people don't tend to slice open those trees to see inside. Walter Shortle does. As a research plant pathologist with the Northeastern Research Station, USDA Forest Service in Durham, New Hampshire, Shortle worked with renowned tree pathologist Alex Shigo, who dissected more than 15,000 trees from 1959 to 1985.

"It's a bad name," says Walter Shortle. "Virtually all of the stem defects that we tend to call 'frost cracks' are caused initially by something other than frost."

Hundreds of those tree dissections were made specifically for the purpose of tracing these so-called frost cracks to their point of origin within the tree. "Every time we've dissected these trees," says Shortle, "we've traced the cracks to some injury or wound. Frost may contribute to cracks—by making them larger—but it's seldom the initial cause."

No matter how cold the winter night, those cracks would not be there without the wound. According to Shortle, cracks begin with almost any kind of injury. Fire scars, logging damage, pruning wounds, rodent gnaw-

ings, deer rubs, even root rot or branch stubs all create areas of weakness. These localized spots of exposed sapwood—not just cracked bark, but openings through to wood—are all it takes to start a crack in the stem. Left open, that exposed sapwood will likely dry and shrink, resulting in small cracks or checks. In time, decay organisms infect cracked wounds, which then become wet.

As Shortle explains, this is when freezing air can become important because when water in that wet wood freezes, it expands. "It is logical that the force of rapid freezing could make the cracks larger," he says. "And that process could repeat itself with repeated events of rapid cooling." With such forces at work, something has to give, and typically it is that weak spot—the first minor crack—that lets go.

When it does, it is often accompanied by a sharp, loud report like a rifle shot echoing through the cold winter night. "That rifle sound is real. Cracking wood does make a loud sound," says Shortle. "We think it is the sound of wood ripping at some previously formed minor crack." In his text, *A New Tree Biology,* Alex Shigo (Shortle's mentor) wrote that "cold temperature may pull the trigger for the crack," but it is some wound that "loads the gun."

But as Shortle is quick to point out, the cracking story does not end there, and freezing is not the only thing that can pull that trigger. "Further enlargement of the crack is likely due to the force of inrolling ribs of wound wood." You've seen these—ridges of odd wood running vertically up the trunk along the edges of a crack or seam. The growth pressure of these ribs, says Shortle, "is a key force in many young, fast-growing trees with small basal wounds." Formation of this wound wood around the initial wound and along the subsequent stem cracks usually leads to wound closure. But not always. Says Shortle, "Sometimes the rib turns inward, keeping the wound aerated and favoring internal rot."

That only worsens the situation. Further enlargement of the crack can then also be caused by wind twisting that already cracked and decay-weakened stem. "A cracked cylinder would not do well twisted," says Shortle. "Sure, you hear those rifle shots on calm, cold nights," he says, "but you may also hear them on windy summer nights and think they are just forked branches breaking off. It could be stems cracking."

This all means that even small and minor wounds can become large and major problems for trees when they are subjected to the forces of drying, freezing, and wind. What begins as just a small nick at the root collar can become a crack or seam extending up the trunk. A flush-cut pruning wound can open a gash in the side of your most prized shade tree, providing an entry court for insects and disease. And all of this can happen even after the initial wound has closed. That's right; a seam in a young tree can close and remain closed for decades before opening again later in the mature stem.

Understanding so-called frost cracks provides yet another reason not to beat up trees. We can't just blame it on frost. If frost really were the cause, wouldn't all the trees in the vicinity of a cracked tree be cracked? "That's the important thing," says Shortle. "Cracks are associated with injuries and infections, which can be controlled, at least in part, by silviculture. We can't control frost, but cracks are caused by wounding, and we can control that." ∽

Bibliography

❧

What the authors are reading

GENERAL REFERENCE

DeGraaf, Richard M., and Mariko Yamasaki. *New England Wildlife: Habitat, Natural History, Distribution*. Hanover, New Hampshire: University Press of New England. 2000.

Thompson, Elizabeth H., and Eric R. Sorenson. *Wetland, Woodland, Wildland: A Guide to the Natural Communities of Vermont*. Lebanon, New Hampshire: University Press of New England. 2000.

AMPHIBIANS

Hunter, Malcolm et al. *Maine Amphibians and Reptiles*. Orono: University of Maine Press. 1999.

Petranka, J.W. *Salamanders of the United States and Canada*. Washington, D.C.: Smithsonian Institution Press. 1998.

BIRDS

Eastman, John, and Amelia Hansen. *Birds of Forest, Yard, and Thicket*. Mechanicsburg, Pennsylvania: Stackpole Books. 1997.

Marzluff, John M., and Tony Angell. *In the Company of Crows and Ravens*. New Haven: Yale University Press. 2005.

Petersen, Wayne, and Roger Burrows. *Birds of New England*. Auburn, Washington: Lone Pine Publishing, 2004.

National Geographic. *Field Guide to the Birds of North America*. Washington, D.C.: National Geographic Society. 2002.

Sibley, David. *The Sibley Field Guide to Birds of Eastern North America*. New York: Knopf. 2003.

Sibley, David. *The Sibley Guide to Bird Life and Behavior*. New York: Knopf. 2001.

Stokes, Donald. *A Guide to the Behavior of Common Birds*. Boston: Little, Brown and Company. 1979.

FLOWERS AND FERNS

Brown, Paul Martin. *Wild Orchids of the Northeastern U.S.* Ithaca, New York: Cornell University Press. 1997.

Dwelley, Marilyn. *Spring Wildflowers of New England*. Camden, Maine: Down East Books. 2000.

Dwelley, Marilyn. *Summer and Fall Wildflowers of New England*. Camden, Maine: Down East Books. 2004.

Newcomb, Lawrence. *Newcomb's Wildflower Guide*. New York: Little Brown. 1989.

Wallner, Jeff, and Mario J. DiGregorio. *New England's Mountain Flowers: A High Country Heritage.* Missoula, Montana: Mountain Press. 1997.

Cobb, Boughton et al. *Ferns of Northeastern and Central North America* (Peterson's Field Guides). New York: Houghton Mifflin. 2005.

GEOLOGY

Little, Richard D. *Dinosaurs, Dunes and Drifting Continents: The Geohistory of the Connecticut Valley.* Greenfield, Massachusetts: Valley Geo Publications. 1986.

Pielou, E.C. *After the Ice Age: The Return of Life to Glaciated North America.* Chicago: University of Chicago Press. 1992.

Van Diver, Bradford B. *Roadside Geology: Vermont and New Hampshire.* Missoula, Montana: Mountain Press. 1987.

Wessels, Tom. *The Granite Landscape: A Natural History of America's Mountain Domes, from Acadia to Yosemite.* Woodstock, Vermont: Countryman Press. 2002.

INSECTS

Brock, Jim P., and Kenn Kaufman. *The Butterflies of North America (Kaufman Focus Guides).* New York: Houghton Mifflin. 2003.

Dunkle, Sidney. *Dragonflies Through Binoculars: A Field Guide to North American Dragonflies.* New York: Oxford University Press. 2000.

MAMMALS

Feldhamer, George A., Bruce C. Thompson, and Joseph A. Chapman , eds. *Wild Mammals of North America: Biology, Management, and Economics.* Baltimore: The Johns Hopkins Press. 1982.

Gibbons, Diane. *Mammal Tracks and Sign of the Northeast.* Lebanon, New Hampshire: University Press of New England. 2003.

Kilham, Ben. *Among the Bears: Raising Orphan Cubs in the Wild.* New York: Owl Books. 2003.

Nelson, Richard. *Heart and Blood: Living with Deer in America.* New York: Knopf. 1997.

RIVERS AND AQUATIC LIFE

Caduto, Michael. *Pond and Brook: A Guide to Nature in Freshwater Environments.* Hanover, New Hampshire: University Press of New England. 1990.

Colburn, Elizabeth. *Vernal Pools: Natural History and Conservation.* Granville, Ohio: McDonald and Woodward. 2004.

Ernst, Lovich et al. *Turtles of the United States and Canada.* Washington, D.C.: Smithsonian Institution Press. 1994.

Johnson, Charles. *Bogs of the Northeast.* Lebanon, New Hampshire: University Press of New England. 1985.

McClane, A.J. *McClane's New Standard Fishing Encyclopedia.* New York: Henry Holt & Co. 1974.

Vogel, Steven. *Life in Moving Fluids.* Princeton: Princeton University Press. 1994.

SHRUBS

Eastman, John, and Amelia Hansen. *The Book of Forest and Thicket: Trees, Shrubs, and Wildflowers of Eastern North America.* Mechanicsburg, Pennsylvania: Stackpole Books. 1992.

Petrides, George A., and Roger Tory Peterson. *A Field Guide to Trees & Shrubs: Northeastern and North-Central United States and Southeastern and South-Central Canada* (Peterson's Field Guides). New York: Houghton Mifflin. 1973.

Symonds, George. *The Shrub Identification Book.* New York: Morrow Quill. 1973.

TREES AND FORESTS

Beattie, Thompson et al. *Working With Your Woodland.* Lebanon, New Hampshire: University Press of New England. 1993.

Connor, Sheila. *New England Natives: A Celebration of People and Trees.* Cambridge, Massachusetts: Harvard University Press. 1994.

Fergus, Charles. *Trees of New England: A Natural History.* Guilford, Connecticut: Globe Pequot Press. 2005.

Heinrich, Berndt. *The Trees in My Forest.* New York: Ecco. 1998.

Peterson, Lee Allen. *Edible Wild Plants: Eastern/ Central North America* (Peterson's Field Guides). New York: Houghton Mifflin. 1977.

Peattie, Donald Culross. *A Natural History of Trees of Eastern and Central North America.* Boston: Houghton Mifflin. 1991.

Symonds, George. *The Tree Identification Book.* New York: William Morrow & Company. 1973.

Wessels, Tom. *Reading the Forested Landscape: A Natural History of New England.* Woodstock, Vermont: Countryman Press. 2004.

OTHER

Cronon, William. *Changes in the Land.* New York: Hill and Wang. 1995.

Heacox, Kim. *The Smithsonian Guide to Natural America—Northern New England (VT/NH/ME).* New York: Random House. 1999.

Marchand, J. Peter. *North Woods.* Boston: Appalachian Mountain Club. 1994.

Miller Jr., Orson. *Mushrooms of North America.* New York: E.P. Dutton. 1987.

Rezendes, Paul. *Tracking and the Art of Seeing.* New York: HarperResource. 1999.

Schaeffer, Vincent A., and John Day. *Field Guide to the Atmosphere* (Peterson's Field Guides). New York: Houghton Mifflin. 1998.

Index

◦

About the Authors

ᕫ

BILL AMOS, a former marine biologist, metamorphosed over the years into an author, bio-photographer, and naturalist who finds every aspect of the living world fascinating. His publications include more than a dozen books, articles for *National Geographic, Scientific American, Reader's Digest,* and other magazines, and newspaper columns. He and his wife, Catherine, occupy what once was a hillside farm in Vermont's Northeast Kingdom.

VIRGINIA BARLOW has been writing and editing at *Northern Woodlands* magazine since it began in 1994. She also is a partner at Redstart Forestry, a forestry consulting company in Corinth, Vermont.

MADELINE BODIN is a freelance writer specializing in wildlife conservation and writes with equal zeal about topics that fascinate her and gross her out. She's written for *Audubon, National Wildlife, The Christian Science Monitor,* and many other publications.

CATHERINE BUNI, former editor and publisher of AMC Outdoors, is a freelance writer and editor. Her writing has been published by *Rock & Ice, Backpacker,* and *Outside,* among others. For Time-Life Books, she wrote *The Greatest Adventures of All Time.* She lives with her two kids and husband on an adventure-packed hilltop in East Montpelier, Vermont.

MICHAEL J. CADUTO is an author, educator, ecologist, and storyteller who once used CPR to save a chipmunk's life. He has written and co-authored fifteen books, including the *Keepers of the Earth* series, *Pond and Brook, Earth Tales from Around the World, Native American Gardening,* and *A Time Before New Hampshire: The Story of a Land and Native Peoples.* Michael's most recent book is a work of fiction called *Abraham's Bind: Bible Stories of Trickery, Folly, Mercy and Love* (SkyLight Paths).

CARRIE CHANDLER is a freelance writer who works as the editorial assistant at *Northern Woodlands* magazine. When not searching for new publications to hound with queries, she enjoys doing anything outside. Although born and raised in Georgia, she loves living in Vermont, but that is subject to change on those extremely cold winter days.

DAVID L. DEEN has been the river steward for the Connecticut River Watershed Council since 1997. He is responsible for protecting the river and its watershed, from the Massachusetts border to the Canadian border. His monthly column, *River Currents,* tells enjoyable stories about the Connecticut River and discusses issues facing it. David serves in the Vermont Legislature and has spent most of his 18 years of service on the Natural Resources or Fish, Wildlife, and Water Resources committees.

STEVE FACCIO is a conservation biologist at the Vermont Institute of Natural Science, where his work focuses on the ecology and long-term monitoring of forest songbirds, vernal pool amphibians, and the recovery and management of Vermont's peregrine falcon population. An accomplished wildlife photographer, his images have appeared in many regional and national magazines, calendars, books, and websites. He lives in the hills of Strafford, Vermont, with his wife and two daughters.

NORAH LAKE is a recent graduate of Dartmouth College, where she majored in environmental studies, earned her teaching certificate, and explored the peaks and valleys of the White Mountains. Her path is wandering circuitously in the direction of teaching kids about the wonders and complexities of nature, whether in the classroom, in the forest, or on the farm.

DAN LAMBERT is the northeast bird monitoring coordinator for the American Bird Conservancy and a research associate at the Vermont Institute of Natural Science. He directs Mountain Birdwatch, a long-term monitoring program for high-elevation songbirds, and has authored several papers and reports on montane and riparian bird communities. Dan enjoys canoeing wild rivers, getting lost in swamps, and exploring woods and streams with his family.

TED LEVIN is a naturalist who has worked for the National Park Service, the Bronx Zoo, and the Montshire Museum of Science. His essays appear in publications as different as *Audubon* and *Sports Illustrated,* among many others. His photographs are published worldwide. In 2004 Levin was awarded the Burroughs Medal for his book *Liquid Land: A Journey Through the Florida Everglades.* His other books include *Backtracking: The Way of a Naturalist* and *Blood Brook: A Naturalist's Home Ground.*

STEPHEN LONG is one of the founding editors of *Northern Woodlands* magazine. He and his wife, novelist Mary Hays, live in Corinth, Vermont, on land they've conserved through the Vermont Land Trust.

ANNE MARGOLIS is a writer and the managing editor of *Northern Woodlands.* She has also worked in alternative energy, outdoor education, and biological research. Anne holds a BA from Dartmouth College in environmental studies with a minor in biology and lives in Corinth, Vermont.

KENT P. MCFARLAND is a research biologist with the Conservation Biology Department at the Vermont Institute of Natural Science (VINS). He came to VINS in 1994, shortly after receiving his Masters degree in biology from Antioch University. It was the bright birds of Paraguay that attracted Kent to field research. After a few months as a Peace Corps volunteer, he bought a cheap pair of binoculars and an Argentinean bird guide and became addicted. His research has taken him throughout the Americas studying and writing about wildlife and conservation.

TII MCLANE is a free-lance forest ecologist living in Strafford, Vermont. Her interest in the forest began with a love for trees and chainsaws and has carried on to include a Peace Corps stint in West Africa, forestry consulting in Vermont, and, more recently, a focus on herbaceous plants and a particular passion for grasses and sedges. In her spare time she plays Appalachian string band music.

ALAN PARKER is a lifelong resident of the Danville, Vermont, area. He's both a gardener and a forest lover, so he has mixed feelings about worms and always returns the unused ones to the garden after fishing expeditions. His work and recreation take him in many directions—carpentry jobs, hunting, active involvement in a local church, and nonprofit work with a particular focus on land conservation.

ROSE PAUL is the director of science and stewardship for the Vermont chapter of The Nature Conservancy. Her work over the last eight years has taken her around the state restoring natural communities, from fens to floodplains to rich northern hardwood forests, on the Conservancy's 46 nature preserves. Rose is part of a national network of conservationists working to restore water quality for the benefit of people and aquatic life, and she can often be found in your local community spreading the word about invasive plant species.

ALAN PISTORIUS is a mostly retired freelance writer and naturalist (that part doesn't retire). He has written, co-written, and edited books on birds and other natural history subjects, farms, and Gil Hodges; periodical pieces have treated of mice and men, moose and milfoil, mosquitos and migration, as well as Rocky Mountain national parks and Wisconsin snakes and Everglades ecology and the economics of the apple-growing industry.

CHRIS RIMMER has been director of conservation biology at the Vermont Institute of Natural Science since 1986. Current research focuses on ecology and conservation of montane forest birds in the Northeast, including recent investigations of mercury burdens in Bicknell's Thrush. He has spearheaded an avian conservation research program on the island of Hispaniola (Dominican Republic and Haiti) since 1994. Rimmer is co-author of the forthcoming *Guide to the Birds of Hispaniola,* to be published by Princeton University Press in the fall of 2006.

MICHAEL SNYDER is a forester in Vermont. His bag is mixed.

CATHERINE TUDISH is a writer and teacher who lives in Strafford, Vermont. Her first book, *Tenney's Landing: Stories*, was published by Scribner in 2005. Her second, a novel, is scheduled to come out in the fall of 2007.

GEOFF WILSON is an educator and facilities manager with the Hubbard Brook Research Foundation, as well as an adjunct faculty member at Plymouth State University, where he teaches biology and natural history courses. He has been involved with the Hubbard Brook Ecosystem Study since 1992, with breaks for graduate school and to serve as a Peace Corps Volunteer in Tanzania. He lives in North Woodstock, New Hampshire, with his wife and son.

JOAN WALTERMIRE is in charge of exhibits at the Montshire Museum of Science in Norwich, Vermont. She lives in Vershire, Vermont.

CHUCK WOOSTER is the associate editor of *Northern Woodlands* magazine, where he has worked since 1998 writing copy, keeping the books, and editing the Wellborn Corner newspaper series. On the side, he runs Sunrise Farm, a small meat and vegetable operation in White River Junction, Vermont. He wrote *Living with Sheep,* published by Lyons Press in 2005.

About the New Hampshire Charitable Foundation

The New Hampshire Charitable Foundation has been working to improve the quality of life in the communities it serves since 1962 by managing a collection of funds that are created by individuals, families, and corporations for charitable purposes. Each year, the Foundation awards millions of dollars in grants to nonprofits and scholarship funds to students. Based in Concord, the Foundation roots itself in communities across the state through its seven regions—Lakes, Manchester, Monadnock, Nashua, North Country, Piscataqua, and the Upper Valley. The Upper Valley regional office was established in 1994 and serves 61 communities in the Connecticut River valley region of west-central New Hampshire and east-central Vermont. For more information, visit www.nhcf.org.

About Northern Woodlands

Northern Woodlands is a non-profit organization based in Corinth, Vermont, whose mission is to encourage a culture of forest stewardship in the Northeast by increasing understanding of and appreciation for the natural wonders, economic productivity, and ecological integrity of the region's forests. *Northern Woodlands* magazine, now in its twelfth year, is delivered to 10,000 subscribers across the region each season, and its companion program, *Northern Woodlands* Goes to School, reaches 5,000 students across Maine, New Hampshire, and Vermont. Northern Woodlands also publishes *The Place You Call Home* series of guides for landowners and syndicates the Wellborn Corner article series to newspapers each week in conjunction with the New Hampshire Charitable Foundation. For more information, visit www.northernwoodlands.org.